WORK LESS,
MAKE MORE

JAMES SCHRAMKO

Printed in the USA

First Edition

National Library of Australia Cataloguing-in-Publication
entry available for this title at nla.gov.au

Title: Work Less, Make More:
The Counter-intuitive Approach to Building a Profitable
Business, and a Life You Actually Love/
James Schramko, author.

ISBN: 978-0-6482060-0-2

Cover Design: Studio1 Design

Interior Design and Layout: Swish Design

For my kids: Jack, Jordan, Jamieson and Jensen.

You were, and continue to be, the motivation behind everything I've achieved in life. I hope this book plays a part in helping you achieve everything you dream of.

WORK LESS, MAKE MORE

The counter-intuitive approach to building a
profitable business, and a life you actually love

JAMES SCHRAMKO

FOREWORD

I first came across James Schramko in 2011 via *Freedom Ocean*, the podcast he co-hosted with Tim Reid. (I was a big fan of Tim's other podcast, *Small Business Big Marketing*, so followed him to *Freedom Ocean*.)

At the time, I was your typical struggling small business owner. My web and graphic design studio was barely breaking even, I was working insane hours to keep things afloat, and my mental health was in tatters.

I was searching for the secret sauce I was sure I was missing out on; the 'one thing' I could do that would make everything magically better. I hoped *Freedom Ocean* would show me what that 'one thing' might be.

Sadly, most of the things James and Tim discussed on the show—advanced internet marketing tips—went straight over my head. They were not the answer to my business woes.

So, I stopped listening and James faded from my consciousness.

Fast forward a few years and he popped up at a conference my husband and I were at. By this point in time, 'my business' had become 'our business' and, while our finances had improved, our workloads were out of control and we were incredibly burnt out.

As James took the stage to present, I despondently picked up my pen, expecting to fill my notebook with tips and ideas I didn't have the skills or time to action.

The James who spoke at that conference was a different cat to the one I'd listened to on *Freedom Ocean*, however.

He told us we were all working too much. (No kidding!) But then he outlined exactly how we could reverse that; providing tips that were actually doable.

Suddenly, I was back on the James bandwagon.

I started listening to his SuperFastBusiness podcast.

I listened to him speak on other people's podcasts.

I noted the advice he offered in a mastermind group we were both part of.

And the editor part of my brain thought, 'He has great stories, proven experience and is one of those rare people who walks the talk. Why hasn't he written a book yet?'

As it turned out, he did have a couple of working manuscripts.

I had a look.

And said to him:

> *'These books are fine, but they'd only appeal to people who already know you. I feel you have ideas and philosophies that can reach (and help) a much wider audience.'*

But, what was the book that could deliver those ideas?

I started trawling through ten years' worth of podcast transcripts. I read countless posts in his SuperFastBusiness forum. I spoke to people whose businesses he'd helped.

I was looking for the big idea or theme that best summed up James' unique approach to business and life. Was it:

- His 'Question Everything' contrarian approach?
- His signature 'Own the Racecourse' philosophy?
- His love of the recurring subscription business model?

Where we got to in the end seems obvious, but belies the sheer number of ideas that had to be discarded first!

Work Less, Make More.

A highly attractive promise. A BIG promise. But one I knew James could deliver on.

Why? Because he's actually doing it. Plus, everything he teaches has been tried and tested. First on himself. Then on the thousands of people he's coached over the years.

This experience allows him to dispense advice with a unique mixture of certainty and compassion.

It's been a rare delight to work with James on this book. It's allowed me to play a part in helping people in a similar position to where my husband and I were three years ago: stressed out and underpaid for the hours we were working.

At that time, one 50-minute presentation combined with a 10-minute mastermind session with James helped us grow our team, make our business more profitable and get our evenings and weekends back. (Our kids particularly appreciated that last one.)

If an hour with James could do that for us, imagine what 20 years of experience compressed into 30,000 words might do for you?

I invite you to turn the page and find out.

Enjoy *Work Less, Make More*.

I look forward to seeing you on the other side.

> Kelly Exeter
> Writer and Editor, kellyexeter.com

CONTENTS

INTRODUCTION
Are you leaving life on the table?

I'm on stage, about to present at a very exclusive conference. There are 50 people sitting in front of me, and they all share a few traits.

They're smart and highly driven.

They've paid thousands of dollars to be here (and so understand the value of investing in themselves and their businesses).

And ... they're *tired*.

Some of them are making decent money, but they're working really hard for it.

As I start to speak, I can see them looking at me thinking I'm going to be yet another guy telling them all the things they can do to make more money. Things that will involve them working *even harder* than they are now.

Then I share with them what my average working day looks like:

I wake up, drink a glass of water, check the surf conditions, have some breakfast, make a coffee, go for a surf, come back home and only then do I sit down at my computer for a few hours and do my highest-level activity. I then have a leisurely lunch, go for another surf, do another focused block of activity, shift my attention to dinner and entertainment, and then it's off to bed.

Yes, that's right. I work just a few hours a day.

At this point I have the room's undivided attention. I'm not the first guy to talk about working less. But I am the first guy they've come across who's actually doing it while making six figures a month. (Yep, a month.)

No #hustle.

No weekly selling webinars or online summits.

No stress-inducing, sleep-depriving, relationship-threatening once-a-quarter product launches.

Just a business model with smooth cash flow, predictable income, and the ability to do work that is meaningful to me.

Of course, life didn't always look like this.

Working for the man

In 1994, I was 23, newly married and working a desk job in a telecommunications company.

A workmate of mine was occupying our spare room at the time, and his average working day looked like this: sleep in every morning, jog down to the beach for a swim, come back, make some phone calls for a bit, then go out with his friends and drink.

He was in sales, making six figures a year.

I was the guy in the office doing all the work, processing his orders and taking home the handsome sum of $35,000.

My wife, on a similar salary, was pregnant. And we were in a bind. We couldn't afford to live on my wage alone when the baby arrived. I needed to double my income—fast. And it was clear the only way to do that was to move into sales.

Unfortunately, the company I worked for liked me right where I was—performing a complex role that'would be difficult to train someone else to do.

I had to look elsewhere.

Having been passionate about cars my whole life, I headed for the car yards. After being rejected by a Toyota dealership, my next port of call was BMW. And after some persuasive talking, I beat 27 applicants for the job, securing my chance to make some tidy commission on top of a very low base salary.

This was the start of a 14-year career in the car dealership industry.

I was good at selling cars.

By the age of 24 I was the number one BMW salesperson in Australia.

By the age of 27 I was working for Mercedes-Benz, and had been in the new car sales guild for high achievers twice. (My second year there, I was number one in Australia.) I was a sales manager at 28, general sales manager at 30, and general manager of an entire dealership by 33.

What set me apart from my peers?

The **first thing** was that I read business books voraciously.

I first picked up Tom Hopkins' *How to Master the Art of Selling* when I was 12. In my 20s I was on to Jay Abraham, Peter Drucker, Dan Kennedy and Gary Halbert, consuming everything they had to offer about growth strategies for business.

The **second thing** was that I actually put those learnings into action.

I measured as many things as I could, creating systems and processes that went with me from dealership to dealership. These allowed me to achieve personal success, and also turn around underperforming dealerships—making them highly profitable. My sales processes were so good Mercedes-Benz asked me to train sales managers from other dealerships in advertising for, hiring and training new salespeople.

The **third thing** was that I was very motivated.

At 31 I was a father of four, and we were servicing two mortgages while living in one of the most expensive cities in the world—Sydney. My number one priority at the time was to provide my family with a comfortable life free from financial stress. Having worked my way up to a salary package of around $300,000 a year at this point, you'd think I'd be saying I achieved that goal.

The truth was, I felt a long way from being financially safe.

The perils of single source dependency

I had a privileged upbringing thanks to my father having a very senior role in the company he worked for. My family lived in the expensive Sydney suburb of Mosman, and I went to an exclusive private boys' school.

While I was at school, the 1980s happened—massive inflation, and interest rates through the roof. But my dad was making great money. My family was fine.

Until the early 90s that is, when a corporate raider bought the company my father worked for, promptly liquidated the assets and made my dad redundant.

My dad's salary couldn't be replaced in the harsh economic climate of the time. Which meant my parents were completely crunched—caught with high interest rates on a big mortgage, a luxury car lease, and a small amount of equity in their home.

This was my first exposure to the perils of single-source dependency.

While it was the way most people did things back then, having all your income coming from one source (a job) is a huge risk.

My parents had to sell the expensive house and car and rebuild their assets from scratch. They did it, but it took decades and incredible resilience on their part.

Fast forward to 2007, and I find myself in a similar situation.

I'm sitting in the lunchroom at work, reading about the problems America is having with the sub-prime lending market and thinking, *If this spreads to Australia and people stop buying luxury cars, I'm not going to fare well.*

I'd negotiated my way to a salary very few dealerships could afford to pay. My family's assets and way of life were completely dependent on that income. Most interestingly, all the systems and processes I'd laid down at my dealership meant it operated like clockwork and could realistically run without me.

If the bottom fell out of the Australian market, I was going to find myself in the same position my dad did all those years ago. The thought of walking into my house one day and explaining to my family that I had no income was haunting.

A job isn't an asset. But a business can be.

In September 2006 I wrote this in a notebook:

MY GOALS ... create automated income so I am independently wealthy and can enjoy my life passionately.

One thing had become abundantly clear well before the financial meltdown. A job, no matter how well it paid, could not provide me with:

- Automated income
- Independent wealth
- The ability to enjoy my life passionately

The business books I'd been reading throughout my twenties also highlighted that having a business was the best way to build an asset.

Time invested in a job was compensated via a capped wage. No matter how hard you worked, the amount you'd make would always have a ceiling on it.

But there was no limit to what you could make from a business. All the rewards of hard work went into your pocket, not someone else's. And a business set up correctly was an asset that could be sold.

For these reasons, I always had some kind of side-business going alongside my jobs in the car industry.

I bought and sold custom number plates with a workmate for a while.

I started an advertising company with an accounting college friend, where we tried to sell premium space in the supermarket to American Express.

I wrote sales copy for a building company to run as newspaper advertisements.

I helped my acting school coach build his school up from 'mired in credit card debt' to a booming, profitable success.

I did several sales training sessions for a financial planner, which I reinvested into buying a new laptop for home.

Somewhere along the way I decided if I was ever going to achieve a level of financial independence where my family never had to worry about money again, I needed to have a business where I was both *creating value* for thousands of people and *getting paid* by thousands of people. That way, if one person was upset and decided they weren't going to pay, no dramas—my income was not entirely dependent on them.

The internet seemed to be the way to achieve this.

Customers were arriving at the showroom knowing more about the new models than Mercedes-Benz were telling us. The travel industry had been revolutionised, and people were making their own bookings instead of going into a travel agency. I was buying CDs online instead of going to a store.

While searching for a Jay Abraham book one day, I found a page that was very compelling. In amongst the bold, italicised and highlighted words, it offered some Jay Abraham reports for free. Once I downloaded those reports, they said I could help other people get them. And if those people happened to buy anything, I would earn a commission.

This seemed very exciting.

It was my first attempt at affiliate marketing, which is essentially being a commission-only sales person for an online business. I thought to myself, *This will be just like selling cars, except I can make sales to hundreds of people at any time of the day or night—even when I'm asleep.*

So, I rolled out my ten feet of internet cable to the phone line, plugged in my laptop and got to work. Over the coming weeks I:

- grabbed my special affiliate link from ClickBank
- built myself a landing page using the free page my internet service provider gave me (it was black with green text)
- put a whole bunch of links to Jay Abraham stuff on there.

Then I sat back and started dreaming about what I'd do with all the money that was about to come gushing into my account.

Except I sold zero.

Not a thing.

I had a lot to learn, and learn I did.

Over the next six years I learned about:

- building websites
- direct response marketing, split testing, writing ad copy and creating e-books
- using Google to place advertisements (AdWords) that would send me customers, and getting Google to rank my website at the top so people would click on my website (SEO).

But perhaps the most important thing I learned was how crucial it was to make the right kind of friends.

You can't become a high achiever if you hang out with low achievers

When I'd just started out in car sales, I was always the first guy at the dealership in the morning. I'd often be sitting there reading my Tom Hopkins *How to Master the Art of Selling* book when the other sales guys came in.

'What are you reading that shit for?' they'd ask.

(They got their answer a year later when I was outselling not only them, but every BMW salesperson in Australia.)

In those early dealership days, books were my way of hanging out with high achievers. When I entered the online world, I continued to learn from the best. I read everything I could get my hands on from the experts at the time—Rich Schefren, Yanik Silver, Perry Marshall, Dan Kennedy, Stephen Pierce, John Carlton, Joe Sugarman, Gary Halbert, Jonathan Mizel, John Reese and others.

The best thing about all these people was that many of them ran events. I got to meet several of them in real life, and some became friends. Not only that, some of the 'regular' people I was meeting and becoming friends with at these events were doing pretty huge things.

One guy was making $100,000 a month as a super-affiliate for a range of products. He'd run ten affiliate campaigns at a time, and inevitably one of them would work really well. Then he'd run another ten. And another ten. He'd keep the campaigns that worked well, and turn off the ones that didn't. It was a simple yet effective approach without too much tech.

By this stage I was achieving some success in the online world. I was an affiliate for XSitePro (software for building websites), and throughout 2006 and 2007 my commissions started to build: from $250/month to $750/month to $1,000/month to $5,000/month.

Then I created an XSitePro cheat sheet. I launched it for $67 and it made $7,000 in the first week.

That's $1,000/day—the same amount my job was making me.

My thought at the time was, *If I can keep this up, I could quit my job.*

The benefits of hanging out with high achievers? They force you to think bigger. They raise the benchmark for what's possible.

Tim, the guy who was earning $100,000 a month, asked me why I was underselling myself.

'Dude, seriously. You're only making $300,000 in a whole year? I make that in less than three months!'

The message was clear. 'If I can do it, you can too.'

I quit my job in 2008

Tim was right. Forget six figures a year. I could make six figures a month, and I went on to do just that.

I'm still doing so today.

But I did it the hard way. (Harder than you'll have to because you have this book.)

In those final years of my life as an employee I was working two shifts—the 8am-7pm shift at the dealership, and then a 9.30pm-3am shift at home. I was pushing hard to make enough money from my online ventures so I could quit the dealership.

As you can imagine, there was no 'living' going on there. I was overweight, pale, stressed, tired and permanently cranky. Some people around me told me I was going to kill myself from exhaustion.

When I quit my job, I was still working like crazy in pursuit of those three key elements from my 2006 notebook:

- Automated income
- Independent wealth
- The ability to enjoy my life passionately

It seemed like I crammed 20 business years into the first five years that followed my dealership days.

But, as you know, I got there in the end. I arrived at the business model I mentioned earlier—the one with *smooth cash flow, predictable income and the ability to do work that's meaningful to me without being a workaholic.*

A large part of that meaningful work is coaching, and over the past nine years I've worked directly with more than 4,000 business owners (and indirectly with several hundred thousand via my podcasts). It's been incredibly fulfilling to help them:

- get where they want to be faster than I did
- avoid the pitfalls I learned about the hard way.
- keep their eye on the prize and avoid distractions.

It's also been nice to be an example of how making good money doesn't have to involve 60-hour work weeks.

Some of my students are posting staggering numbers today, and this makes me happy. Not just because they're 'rich', but because money gives them freedom:

- from doing things they don't really like doing. (They can now hire people to do those things, both in their businesses and their homes.)
- from stress, because there's no single source dependency in their lives. (It's okay if one income stream ceases to exist because they have others.)
- to take on passion projects that make no money at all.

Most of my students are still on an upward journey, of course. But they're making enough money to live well, reduce their debt significantly, and create financial buffers that protect them from disasters. And they no longer work nights and weekends, which means they have time to:

- look after their health
- hang out with the people they love
- pursue the things that interest them.

They're not leaving life on the table anymore.

Three things I'm guessing about you

First, you're probably working too hard for your money.

I can say this with a fair degree of certainty because it's been true for every person I've ever coached. And chances are you wouldn't be reading this book if you spend your days lying on a beach in the Bahamas, living comfortably off a trust fund.

Second, you're miles ahead of where I was when I first started seeking financial independence.

The level of information you can access for free and the tools you have at your disposal today are second to none. (You're definitely not trying to hand-code a website in HTML like I was in 2005.)

Third, you're probably overwhelmed.

All that information is as much a curse as it is a blessing. There are thousands of tools out there that might just be the 'game changer' you've been waiting for. There are thousands of 'gurus' with 'proven systems' and rock-bottom stories offering 'shortcuts to success'. Every life on social media is so airbrushed it's impossible to tell who's full of shit and who isn't.

So, how can I help you? After all, your time and energy are limited. Is there just one thing you can focus on that will help you get your life back?

I think there is.

The metric that matters

To work less and make more, all you need to do is move the needle on one metric: Effective Hourly Rate (EHR).

Here's how to calculate your EHR:

1. Take the amount of revenue you make in a month and subtract your costs. What you have left is your monthly profit. (If you have a job, then your wage is your profit.)

2. Divide your profit by the number of hours you worked in the month to get it.

The number you have now is your EHR.

Let's say you make $20,000 a month in revenue, and your fixed and variable costs come to $15,000. That means your profit will be $5,000. If you work 250 hours a month to achieve that profit then:

$$\$5,000/250 = EHR \ \$20/hour$$

Have you calculated your EHR yet? If you haven't, now is a good time to do it. Make a note of it, along with today's date, because we're about to make some changes.

If your EHR is around $20/hour like my example, don't stress. I've seen that number many times before. And I'm sure I'll keep seeing it, given how many entrepreneurial types discover they have an EHR of less than $10/hour.

So, the 'average' work week is considered to be around 40 hours, (roughly 173 hours per month). We know many people work a lot more than that. Some entrepreneurs brag about working more than 300 hours a month.

Now consider this: If you're working 60 hours a week and have a family or a partner, they won't see much of you because you're working nights and weekends. You probably don't have the time to exercise or eat properly either, so your health may also be suffering.

Furthermore, an EHR in the range of $20/hour means you'll always be struggling to achieve financial independence— the mental freedom that comes from never having to worry about money.

Here's where I'm going to suggest something quite counter-intuitive.

I'm going to ask you to immediately reduce your work hours (gasp). Why?

Because it's very hard to find the energy and mental space you need to increase your revenue if you're working long hours day in and day out.

Right now, working fewer hours might seem impossible. That's okay. This book will show you how eliminating certain activities while building your health will ensure your life becomes both easier and more profitable.

Now, back to that first EHR calculation we did.

Let's say that after reading just a fraction of this book you manage to increase your monthly revenue to $25,000 a month while keeping your fixed and variable costs the same ($15,000). Your profit is now $10,000. And if you *focus only on the things that matter and generate profit*, and drop anything that doesn't, you should be able to reduce your work hours from 250/month to ~160/month.

$10,000/160 = EHR $62.50/hour

You're now making three times more per hour working 90 hours less per month!

And you're on your way.

When you're only working 160 hours a month, you'll be amazed at how much energy you have and how clear your thinking becomes. From there, it's not a huge jump to build your monthly revenue to $40,000 while your fixed and variable costs rise slightly to $20,000. (The extra costs will likely be a mix of hiring a team or buying more marketing.) Your profit will become $20,000.

Let's say you now reduce your working hours a little more, because you have better systems in place and are enjoying life more. Now you're working 130 hours a month (roughly six hours a day, five days a week; or five hours a day, six days a week).

$20,000/130 = EHR $154/hour

This is where life starts getting really great. You're making more money, working fewer hours, seeing more of your family, and you even have time for a fun hobby. (Remember fun? Remember hobbies?)

You're also sleeping better, which translates to a clearer head and better productivity when you're working.

Now, let's take your clearer head and improved energy levels (along with this book), and channel them into creating a product or service that generates $100,000 per month.

The key figures will now look something like this:

- $100,000 a month in revenue
- fixed and variable costs of around $40,000
- profit of $60,000

By now you'll only be working 100 hours a month because you have a great team and great systems in place.

$60,000/100 = EHR $600/hour

If an EHR of $600/hour or more seems unbelievable to you right now, that's okay. I never thought I'd be seeing numbers like that either. But it's actually typical of what many of my students have been able to achieve. And it's certainly how I live my life now.

Best of all, we get to choose our work hours. We can work 7-8 hour days, three days a week. Or 4-5 hour days, five days a week. Because we can choose our work hours, *we can choose to work when our energy levels are highest.* Which means when we're on, we're on. And when we're off, we get to actually relax and enjoy life.

Increasing your EHR to this level is a learnable and repeatable process. If you read this book and take action along the way, I promise you will experience some powerful EHR transformations.

Is EHR the only metric when it comes to running a profitable business that lets you live a life you actually love?

No, it's not.

But it is the most useful metric in the context of how to measure change as a result of reading this book.

My promise to you

I could tell you how I've helped clients become multi-millionaires, put together incredibly lucrative triangulation deals and brokered some great joint ventures.

I could tell you about the high-flyers I'm now friends with, and how 'the sky's never the limit' when it comes to what you can earn.

I could make some huge promises based on what I've helped other people achieve.

But I don't want this book to be aspirational fluff that gets you thinking, 'One day I'll be able to …'

I want you to take action at the end of every chapter.

With that in mind, let me give two examples of just how easy it is to positively impact your EHR.

ONE: You're probably doing something in your business right now that's taking up a fair amount of your time, yet you're struggling to see the benefits. (I can almost guarantee it involves a prominent social media platform.) But you keep doing it either because other people said you should, or because 'everyone else is doing it', or you never thought about why you do it at all.

Stop doing that thing right now. (Or at least limit it to one hour per day.)

Result: Not only has your EHR just increased, you'll also feel relief at not having to persist with it any longer.

TWO: Perhaps you have 'that client' or 'that product' or 'that project'. Someone or something tedious that consumes far more resources than you get in return for your effort.

Drop it.

Result: Now you have more time for the *great* clients/products/projects.

Do these two things sound too easy?

I'm only just getting started!

Head over to Chapter 1. It's time to ramp up your personal effectiveness.

CHAPTER 1
Personal Effectiveness

In Japan, the word *karoshi* means 'death from overwork'. It's estimated that *karoshi* causes around 1,000 deaths per year, and almost 5% of Japan's stroke and heart attack fatalities in employees below 60 years of age.

Which is why I can't understand people talking about working 19-hour days like it's a badge of honour.

Working too much turns you into a blunt instrument. An effective work day is about energy management, not time management. You need to shift your thinking towards doing less and feeling totally okay about it.

And the best way to change your focus is to increase how *effective* you are.

Notice I didn't say 'how *productive* you are'.

A lot of people obsess about productivity, which is all about getting through a lot in a given period of time. If

Everything you'll have in the future comes down to what you'll do as a result of what you learn from this moment in time onwards.

you're being productive doing the wrong things, however, you'll be doing a lot, yet remaining in the same spot. Like a hamster on a wheel.

It's time to shift your focus to doing the right things.

The beauty of the changes I'm about to step you through is they'll all have a positive impact on your EHR before you make any changes to your business operations.

Now that's what I call *effective*.

Step 1: Look in the mirror

If you'd like to know who's responsible for your future, look in the mirror.

Everything you've got today is the sum of everything you've done and everyone you've known to this point.

Everything you'll have in the future comes down to what you'll do as a result of what you learn from this moment in time onwards.

So, step up and take that personal responsibility (if you haven't already).

If your concept of getting ahead in life relies on buying lottery tickets each week and hoping for a big win, you need to re-read those last few paragraphs. You have more chance of being struck by lightning. Twice. Your big win is possible without winning the lottery. Accept this, embrace this, and get ready for your life to change for the better.

(And whenever you need a reminder, take a quick look in the mirror again.)

Step 2: Track your time

Since you've already done the EHR calculation, you know how many hours you're working a week. Which raises my next question: where are you spending those hours?

- Are you on social media for most of the day? (A disturbing number of people spend more than five hours a day on social media and justify it by calling it 'networking', 'researching' or 'marketing'.)
- Are you continuously performing email inbox triage? (More on that in a second.)
- Are you spending a lot of time doing seemingly urgent yet unimportant tasks?

If you're not sure how you spend your time each day, install time management software on your computer. There are good free tools that will email you a summary each week of how many hours you've been on your computer.

My goal is to keep my computer time under 20 hours per week. If your report shows you're putting in 60, 70, 80 or even 100 hours a week, you're running on burnout mode. The number may shock you at first, but the whole point of this book is to help you get your number (whatever it is) down to where you want it to be.

Not everything important in life can be measured so accurately. So take advantage of the fact that time can be tracked. Track your hours, figure out where you're spending them unnecessarily, be honest about it, and make the adjustment.

Then watch your weekly work hours drop, and your EHR climb.

Step 3: Manage your inbox better

Your email inbox is a to-do list that other people get to add to. Be especially careful about subscribing to email newsletters—it means you've now committed future time towards reading or screening those emails.

As soon as you start tracking your activities, you'll almost certainly find you spend more than ten hours a week on email. That's quite a lot. Here are a few tips you can implement now to save you a lot of time in the long term.

Use Gmail as your email provider

Gmail is very good for sorting your emails and filtering out spam. It's also got labels and rules to take care of the emails you want to see and action. It then stores and archives everything for easy searching. The priority for emails you need to read are ones requiring action. News-related emails (i.e. read-only, no action required) should be filtered for you to review at a later date.

*Few things are so urgent
they need an instant reply.
Be the master of your
electronic devices,
not a slave.*

Turn off alerts

Do you really need an email alerting you that someone just tagged you on Facebook? Especially given you're already logging into Facebook 20 times a day and will see the alert when you log in?

Same goes for all other social media platforms.

Turn off email alerts. (And while you're there, turn off push notifications on your phone too.) The absence of alerts will give you an oasis of calm to perform higher value work without interruption.

Switch your phone to silent mode. Few things are so urgent they need an instant reply. Be the master of your electronic devices, not a slave. Attend your phone when it suits you rather than letting it summon you every time someone sends a message or wants to speak with you.

Unsubscribe

Chances are you've subscribed to many email newsletters because you bought something, belong to a program of some kind, or simply want to 'see what they're doing'. I can tell you what they're doing—they're sucking up your hours. (And more than likely trying to sell you things.)

When it comes to emails, there are two main types of people, those who consume and those who create.

I encourage you to create.

Remember, the one who sends the email is the one making the money. The one who receives the email is the one spending the money.

You might think spending hours in your inbox every week looking at the latest and greatest shiny objects—a new course, a free this or a free that—is harmless. The thing is, they're not free. If you have an EHR of $100/hour, and you spend an hour looking at a free course, it just cost you $100 of opportunity. What's more, it's breaking your attention and reducing your effectiveness.

Here's how to unsubscribe from emails quickly. Go to your inbox, and type 'unsubscribe' in the search bar to bring up every newsletter you've subscribed to. Go through them one by one and ask, 'Is this subscription moving me forward in my business, or just taking time from me?' Unsubscribe from any newsletter that isn't taking you and your business forward.

Set up a help desk

How much time do you spend on customer support? If it's 'a lot', a help desk is key to scaling it.

One of my early internet businesses had hundreds of customers. In the beginning, I was the support person those customers could contact via email. Having customer support emails coming into an email address doesn't scale, and consumes a lot of your time.

So, I set up an online help desk (using proper help desk software). Then I hired someone to help me answer those support tickets. Eventually I built a team of six people whose job it was to answer those tickets.

The important thing was, those help requests weren't arriving in my inbox—they were being handled by the help desk software in a central online location. Anyone in our team could access this portal and answer customers. It was no longer me.

Step 4: Set up some bumpers

One day I took my kids and cousins ten-pin bowling. My then 13-year-old son asked for bumpers to be set up when it was his turn. As you know, the objective in bowling is to knock down all the pins. By setting up bumpers, my son eliminated the possibility of losing his ball down one of the gutters. Unsurprisingly, he dominated.

With my own students and my own business, we set up business plans in 12-week blocks. We identify a target, such as adding a new product or service, and then we set up bumpers to keep us on track. Our bumpers are very simple. If something comes along to distract us (a collaboration, joint venture request, podcast interview or request for a new service) we just say, 'Let's review that request at the end of the 12 weeks'.

At the end of 12 weeks we will have effectively knocked down all the pins. We then review available opportunities

In life, we need to set up filters. And one of the best filters is the word 'No'.

and requests before setting up the next lot of pins (our plans/goals for the next 12-week block).

This keeps everyone focused on the key objective, and ensures we deliver on it before moving on to another one.

Step 5: Set up filters

When I'm on a ferry in Sydney Harbour and the seas are big, a wave occasionally crashes over the bow and drenches everything. But that's okay, because I'm inside the ferry. The window acts as a filter between me and the water, so I don't get wet.

In life, we need to set up filters. And one of the best filters is the word 'No'.

Many of us feel obliged to say 'Yes' to everything, even though the reality is we simply can't. We don't have infinite capacity. We need to consider the fact we've got around 180 effective hours per month. If we keep saying 'Yes' to everything it saps our energy, and leaves no power available for the things we'd really like to say 'Yes' to.

We need to say 'Yes' to the things we love, that bring us joy, and are giving us the result we'd like to get. We need to say 'No' to the things we simply don't want to do.

We achieve this by putting up filters.

For example, when I was running the car dealership we had filters for how we bought cars. Some cars sold quickly, while others were much harder to sell. Some colours made a better profit than others. We used this information to create a stock matrix, and this became our filter. Whenever someone came to us with a car to trade in, we could quickly decide whether or not to pay more for it by checking the filter. It was like the answer sheet a teacher uses to mark tests.

Are there filters you can create in your business to make decision making easier? Use them.

Step 6: Time block

My grandfather (and one of my earliest employers) taught me, 'pay yourself first'. This means making sure you look after yourself before you extend yourself to others. Why? Because if you can't look after yourself, you aren't going to be much use to anyone else.

So block time for yourself into your calendar right now.

Guard that time for your deep work.

These time blocks can be at whatever time suits you: from early in the morning to late at night, any day of the week.

The most effective time to block is whenever you feel the most motivated and energised. It's time to throw out the convention of nine to five, Monday to Friday. Some of my most inspired work has been done very early, very late, on weekends, and even while travelling. It's important to only do your deep work when you're feeling really into it. Doing a half-baked work session yields a very low harvest.

If you only work when you're fully engaged you'll be more effective. There are numerous tests showing that students who sleep beat those who cram.

Once your deep work time is blocked, you can let others infiltrate your schedule.

I make myself unavailable for people on Monday, Tuesday, Thursday, Friday, Saturday and Sunday. The only day people can book me through my scheduler is Wednesday. And even then I'm only available for three hours in the morning and three in the afternoon.

So in any given week I'm available to the public for roughly six hours. That's one day for everyone else, and six days for me. But they always have my full concentration during my calls because I've committed that time for others. And my reward is six days off.

What's more, people only get to access those six hours once they've passed through my filters. If someone invites me to be on their podcast, my team will check the podcast before letting that person book through my scheduler. And if someone's applying to join SilverCircle (my high-level mastermind), I'll have a quick email chat with them first and then send a link to my scheduler.

Remember, my scheduler is only available to people who've already been filtered. And when they get there, they can only book times that suit both them and me. It eliminates the back-and-forth of setting up appointments by email,

What happens after a year of 'one high-impact thing for the week'? You get a lot of progress.

and most scheduling tools can adjust for time zones and send a calendar reminder.

To keep calls on track, it's always a good idea to set a mutually agreed objective at the start of the call. If someone seems to be overstaying the allotted time, just mention that you have another call shortly and encourage them to rebook for the following week.

If you're just getting started with this, it doesn't have to be this extreme. Start small.

For example, if you're taking phone calls all day, every day (and especially if they're cutting into your family time or fun pursuits) then turn your phone off between 9am and 12 noon. Make yourself available for calls in the afternoons only. You'll be amazed how quickly people adjust their expectations of your availability once you put stronger boundaries in place.

Step 7: Focus

Think of a camera. You could have a great lens, but unless you're focused on one object, everything is blurry.

Which is why I ask my highest-level students, 'What one high-impact thing will you focus on between now and next week's call?' They tell me, and everything immediately gets simpler.

And what happens after a year of 'one high-impact thing for the week'? You get a lot of progress.

Having a single focus is extremely powerful.

Step 8: Sleep, eat, move

In 1942, more than 80% of Americans slept seven or more hours a night. Today, 40% sleep six hours or less. Thanks to all the devices, games and artificial lights in our lives, we're just not getting enough sleep.

I was one of those sleep-deprived adults—working in a car dealership and raising a family of six while paying off two mortgages and a share portfolio. I was working way too hard, getting too little sleep, and starting to put on weight.

You might be interested to know that I've lost 45 pounds in recent years simply from sleeping more, eating better and surfing every day.

How do you get more sleep? Set an alarm as a reminder to stop work and go to bed. And keep your devices away from where you sleep.

How do you drop weight? Forget the fancy pills or crazy diets. (If you need energy drinks or nootropics to get your work done, you're doing it wrong.)

Just ask yourself: If you were an Olympic athlete, would you be eating chips and drinking Coca-Cola every day? No, you wouldn't. You'd be eating healthy meals because you want to maximise your chances of winning the race and getting the prize money.

In business, if you become a high-performance machine with what you're eating, then you're going to get high-performance results. But if you're overweight, drinking sugary drinks and taking pills that supposedly make up for the nutrients you're missing out on, you're not a high-performance machine.

Eat better from today. It's not optional.

And move. Just a 20 or 30-minute walk every day can bring you out of an unhealthy situation (if you're someone who's currently not moving at all). Find an activity you like doing, and do it every day.

Me, I love surfing. It involves a huge range of muscles, and it's a low-impact sport so it doesn't destroy my body. And it's extremely fun. I mainly do it for the fun, and the health benefits are a happy by-product. I surf each day, sometimes until I'm exhausted. The conditions are always different. As counter-intuitive as it seems, it recharges me, and I always feel a million dollars afterwards. It also helps me sleep very well.

So, move every day. I guarantee it will boost your personal effectiveness.

If you want to get really advanced, you can also get your DNA analysed. It will help you understand who you really are. Once you know your muscle type and recovery rates, food sensitivities and health pre-dispositions, you can plan your food and exercise better.

Humans tend not to purge. We add and add but never subtract.

Step 9: Purge

Nature purges all the time. Storms and fires ravage forests, and from them we get new beginnings. Trees grow back, they revitalise.

Humans tend not to purge. We add and add but never subtract.

How much crap is sitting on your hard drive right now? Is your computer running slow because it's full of junk you don't use? What about all those apps you bought on a whim and never logged into more than twice?

And that's just your computer. What about your office? Is there junk everywhere—pens, papers, Post-it notes, screens, cables, cords, books? All this stuff is taking up energy just looking at it.

It's time to do a big purge.

Start with your office environment: delete, dump, sell or donate.

Next should be your wardrobe, then your garage, then every room in your house. Get a copy of The Life-Changing Magic of Tidying Up. Apply it.

After that, take a look at the people you spend time with. Given you become like the people you spend time with, perhaps some of your friends need to be purged too.

Reduce the things and people in your life down to only those you love and bring you happiness.

Step 10: Create routines

The floorboards in my local coffee shop are worn into a path. Routine is evident in those floorboards—the serving staff travel back and forth along them the same way every day. It saves them time and energy. If they chose a different route every time, they wouldn't be as effective.

All the things in your life that you do every day—exercise, eating well, doing deep work, spending time with your family, housework—should have a routine built around them. Routines free you from the need to negotiate with yourself to get things done. Routines let you operate on auto-pilot and reduce mental clutter in the same way we get dressed each day without questioning whether we should or not.

If you have a negative routine, replace it with a better one. The way we think determines the way we act. And the way we act affects the results we get. So if your actions aren't getting you what you want, change your thoughts. Replace sub-optimal thoughts with better ones.

Routines underpin habits and free up energy—energy you can direct towards being more effective during work periods, and more relaxed during downtime.

Chapter 1 Action Items

- ❑ Install time management software on your computer.

- ❑ Monitor how you're spending your time.

- ❑ Adjust your workflow based on the report.

- ❑ Turn off all social media notifications (both emails and push notifications on your phone).

- ❑ Switch your phone to silent.

- ❑ Unsubscribe from any email newsletter that isn't taking your business forward.

- ❑ Get support emails out of your inbox by using dedicated help desk software.

- ❑ Block 'deep work' time into your calendar (at whatever time suits you) so you have uninterrupted work time.

- ❑ Make portions of your time available to others using a scheduler tool. (The rest of the week is yours.)

- ❑ Purge unwanted things and people from your life.

- ❑ Set a 12-week goal and stick to it. Hint: Actioning items in this book will change your life. Commit 12 weeks to actioning the key elements at the end of each chapter.

- ❏ Prioritise sleep. Get eight hours a night for a week (even if it means not getting as much 'work' done) and see how it feels.

- ❏ Clean up your diet. Eat food that's as close to the source as possible (i.e. not out of packets).

- ❏ Find a type of exercise or daily movement you enjoy, and carve out time to do it every day.

MORE READING/LISTENING

Visit JamesSchramko.com for a secret bonus chapter plus a list of recommended resources and additional notes that expand on this topic.

CHAPTER 2
Planning and Goalsetting

When you're busy taking care of business, it can easily take you for a ride. You know you're on this ride when you become very reactive—constantly putting out fires and responding to whichever customer or product is screaming loudest for your attention.

This is how most people are when they come to me for help. They're so caught up in the day-to-day *doing* that they've lost sight of where they're *going*.

Why planning is important

When I go surfing, it's tempting to jump on the first wave that comes along. If I do, I may well get a half-decent ride. But if I can wait a few more seconds there will often be a better-shaped wave just behind it. Riding the better wave will be more satisfying, and take me closer to where I want to be as a surfer.

In business, opportunities are like waves. They come along all the time. Always jumping on the opportunity right in front of you will see you spending a lot of valuable time on things that aren't your core business. (This also decimates your EHR.)

Worse, you'll be missing opportunities that can take your business where you want it to go.

This is why planning is important. It allows you to decide what type of opportunities you want so you can recognise them when they arrive. Planning also gives you the space and time you need to give these opportunities your all when they arise.

Clearing your brain

If your business was about to crash to the ground and you could only execute one idea, what would it be?

I'd recommend starting with whatever's working for you already.

That's easy to say, but harder to do.

Why? Because most entrepreneurial types find it hard to execute 'just one idea'. They have a million in their head at any one time, and keep adding to them by the day. Those ideas create a lot of noise, clog up the brain's processing capacity, and provide an easy avenue for distraction.

Escape from boredom is a serious enemy of focus.

When I was in my late 20s, it felt like my brain was always so full of information I needed to clear it. I found that a pen, some paper and a bit of quiet time at the breakfast table was a great way to purge all that information.

Purging those ideas doesn't mean getting rid of them forever, or saying you'll never pursue them. You're simply getting them out of your head *for now*.

Here's how to do it:

1. Using a whiteboard or a big sheet of paper, write down everything that's on your mind. Don't stop until you can't think of anything else to write.

2. Take a photo of your whiteboard or piece of paper and file it away for safekeeping.

3. See if you can delete or cross out any items that aren't worth worrying about—ever.

4. Score the remaining items according to their impact (i.e. how important or urgent they are to your mission).

5. Circle the top three items that must remain in your sphere of focus, and transfer them (in order of importance) to your daily action pad, a Post-it note on your workspace, your refrigerator, or whatever.

You can now safely clean the whiteboard, or tear up/shred/bin that piece of paper. And with your head now freed from all those ideas, you can start thinking about where you want to go.

All that attending, consuming and buying means they're burning up so much energy they never implement or execute anything.

The three layers of planning

When I'm working with coaching clients to get them on track and moving forward, we work through three layers of planning:

Layer One: Goal setting

I often see people go to event after event after event. Webinar after webinar after webinar. Course after course after course. And two years later, all they've achieved is having attended those things.

All that attending, consuming and buying means they're burning up so much energy they never implement or execute anything. In fact, they become so overloaded they don't even know where to start.

This is where I find the railway metaphor useful.

Imagine you're at Grand Central Station, and you want to get somewhere.

Maybe that 'somewhere' is starting a new business. Or achieving a significant profit change for your existing business. You may want to build a few days off into your weekly schedule, travel somewhere exciting, or have time to develop a new skill such as cooking.

Whatever it is, close your eyes and really imagine it. Walk around in your future reality. Take in the sights, sounds, smells, tastes and textures. Get intimate with the idea.

Next, make sure you're happy with it.

- Are you happy with the constraints that come with this future reality?
- Are you comfortable with the associated risks?
- Do you know someone else experiencing that kind of reality? What kind of life do they have? Do you want that life?
- Are you prepared to pay the price and do whatever it takes to create this future reality?

Remember, very little ever comes without effort or input. You will need to expend energy to get results.

Now that you know where you want to go, and what it might be like, you can lay down tracks along the easiest and most direct path to the next station.

Layer Two: Time blocking, scheduling and checking in

Often, I see people set the goals for their plan and then kind of stop. It's as if they believe they can achieve their goals simply by having them.

Going back to the train and tracks metaphor, knowing where you want to go won't actually get you there. You need to both lay down some tracks and then roll your train along those tracks.

You may be familiar with Eisenhower's Urgent/Important Matrix:

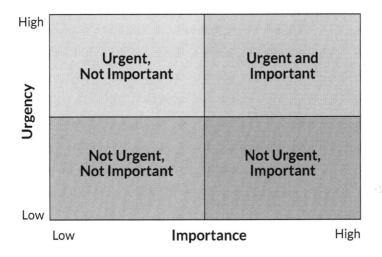

Laying down the tracks to our destination falls in the 'Not Urgent, Important' quadrant—the quadrant people only go to when they 'have time'.

To 'have time' for these activities, we must make time for them.

A powerful way to do it is to block out the time in our calendars. We're effectively 'paying' ourselves by reserving the time we need before others have a chance to take it.

Deadlines are also useful for ensuring you get things done. Parkinson's Law states that 'work expands to fill the time available for its completion'. Therefore, having lots of short deadlines to focus on high-impact activities will increase the effectiveness of what you do.

*When people
expect you to show up,
you make things
happen.*

When I set the date for a live event, that's a deadline. I have no choice but to have everything organised for that date. It's the same if you're travelling to another country. The flight is booked for a specific date, and you need to get packed and to the airport with your passport and all the documents you need before the plane takes off.

I do regular training calls in my coaching programs that involve me sharing specific insights. That's a deadline.

When people expect you to show up, you make things happen.

In my highest-level coaching community, I check in with my students once a week on a group call. That weekly tune-up is fantastic because we can really plot what they're doing well, and where they're getting great results. And seeing each other setting goals and deadlines, and getting things done, encourages them all.

Having 40 to 50 check-ins a year is far more effective than having two or three live events where people fly in, spend a day or two talking about their business, then disappear and get sucked back into life.

These frequent check-ins force you to re-visit your progress as you move along the tracks. If you're straying, you can quickly get back 'on track'. And by measuring and plotting your progress you'll know you're taking the most direct route.

So make sure you set a weekly calendar reminder to check your progress.

Layer Three: Major reviews every 12 weeks

The third layer of planning is having a major review point every 12 weeks.

These reviews are like stations you can stop at along the way. They're milestones where you can celebrate your success, and use as motivation to keep you moving forward to your ultimate destination. You can also check whether your original plan still makes sense, and clarify what the next station looks like so you can lay the tracks to get there.

For example, if your final destination is a business that makes $20,000 a month in recurring income and lets you work no more than 30 hours a week, then your first station may be:

- identifying a market of hungry buyers
- creating or sourcing a product or offer you can sell to them
- building a website page or flyer ready for potential prospects.

It's important to limit the 'distance' between each station to 12 weeks. People often make a plan and then give themselves a year to execute it. When do they do all their execution? Usually in the final month, if not the final weekend. Parkinson's Law in action.

Shortening timelines forces you to be direct, and removes a lot of the 'analysis paralysis' that can stop perfectionist types in their ... well, tracks.

If you want a visual incentive, chart your progress by colouring in a bar graph or using magnets on a whiteboard.

Fun fact: In my first year as a sales professional selling BMWs I'd stick a magnetic Troll Doll on the refrigerator for every car I sold each month. As my skills improved, I had to buy more troll dolls. My system was highly visual and quite fun.

Creating solid systems around planning and goal setting is essential. The systems keep you honest and, most importantly, let you closely track the metrics that are important to you (which for this book is your EHR).

Chapter 2 Action Items

- ☐ Clear your brain. Purge everything from your mind, delete anything that won't have an impact, score the highest impact ones, and transfer the top three. File the rest away somewhere safe. Then forget about them (for now).

- ☐ Figure out your destination: identify your ideal future reality.

- ☐ Lay down the tracks: figure out the steps that will take you to your destination.

- ☐ Create stations along the way at 12-week intervals. These milestones will provide the momentum to keep going.

- ☐ Block out time in your schedule to execute the plan.

- ☐ Set an alert to check your progress weekly.

- ☐ Create a 12-weekly review point.

MORE READING/LISTENING

Visit JamesSchramko.com for a secret bonus chapter plus a list of recommended resources and additional notes that expand on this topic.

CHAPTER 3
Focus and the Power of 64:4

Thomas Jefferson once said, 'There is nothing more unequal than the equal treatment of unequal people'.

When it comes to business, there's nothing more unequal than the equal treatment of unequal business activities.

When you make a to-do list, you're treating all your business tasks equally. You're saying that 'create content' is just as important as 'develop sales offer' when in fact one of them could reward you significantly more. (The second one, in case you're wondering.)

With regular to-do lists we tend to gravitate towards the easiest tasks. We want that little dopamine hit of crossing them off. But the easiest tasks are seldom the most rewarding for our business.

Beware of the unweighted to-do list.

Here's what you should do instead.

I mentioned Eisenhower's Urgent/Important Matrix in Chapter 2.

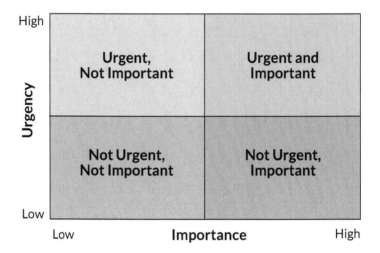

Here's how you use it:

- Start by sketching the matrix up on a large sheet of paper or a whiteboard.
- Next, write each task on your current to-do list on a separate Post-it note.
- Now stick each Post-it note (task) in the most appropriate quadrant on your sheet of paper or whiteboard.

Did you find most of the tasks on your to-do list are neither urgent nor important? Most people do.

Finally, peel off the Post-it notes one at a time and put them into a pile with the highest impact tasks on the top.

To me, this is the most effective way to prioritise tasks. It also encourages the long-lost art of single-tasking.

If you only have one thing to do, doing it becomes easier

As I said earlier, one of my favourite techniques for getting the highest impact results for my coaching students is to give them one thing to do per week. During our weekly check-in call, I ask whether they did that one thing, and what they're going to do next week.

Doing it 50-odd times a year gets some serious results.

Single-tasking is incredibly powerful, as is being able to filter what we're doing and focus only on what will have the greatest impact at that moment in time.

One of my first jobs was as a debt collector. When doing that role I used a program that displayed only one customer at a time. I'd call the customer, make a note of what happened, and then hit Enter to bring up the next one. I could make 170 phone calls per day using that system.

Set up your workflow and environment so you can only work on one thing at a time. And then reward yourself as you move along the track.

If you focus on creating something for 50 minutes, do a non-work activity as a reward. Fifty minutes of focused creation a day adds up to more than 25 hours a month. Given you're

*4% of what
you do generates
64% of your results.
How wild is that?*

probably spending zero hours on truly focused work right now, 25 hours is a significant improvement.

Introducing 64:4

According to the Pareto principle (aka the 80/20 rule), 20% of the invested input is responsible for 80% of the results obtained.

If you take it one step further and apply the rule to itself, 4% of what you do generates 64% of your results.

How wild is that?

Isn't it liberating to know you can coast by doing very few things **as long as they're the right things and you're doing them well?**

Most of my clients are working more than 60 hours a week when they first come to me. We usually discover they can immediately reduce that to 30 hours a week and still make the same income. They're relieved when I help them identify what they can do *less* of, rather than what they should do *more* of.

That was certainly the case with Jarrod.

A 64:4 case study

I met Jarrod Robinson in 2015 and was immediately impressed. He's a very switched on guy. He was highly motivated and very hard working—much like the person I expect to be reading this book.

I'll never forget sitting with Jarrod as he told me everything he was doing.

He was a full-time Physical Education (PE) teacher and had a website/blog called The PE Geek. He started monetising the site by selling an e-book. Then he made this connection:

If one product = good

Then many products = better

So he went from one e-book to eight. He got each one translated into three languages, giving him 24 e-books all up.

Then he started building iPhone apps. One app quickly became 60. He turned 20 of them into Android apps. While some did well, most didn't. But Jarrod didn't care because:

Many products = better

You'd think that 24 e-books and 80 apps would be enough. But not for Jarrod. He built four software-as-a-service (SaaS) products, each requiring a minimum investment of $30,000.

He also had a workshop product that was popular around the world. He'd fly overseas on weekends to deliver his workshop, and then fly home in time for school to start on Monday.

Are you tired yet? Because Jarrod wasn't.

He produced ten video courses.

He launched a podcast and quickly reached 40 episodes.

He created a t-shirt range because … well, why not? Teachers need t-shirts, right?

He created a comic book.

Finally, he created his pièce de résistance—a music album. For teachers.

And he did it all while working full-time as a PE teacher—a job that involved a four-hour daily commute.

When he finished telling me all this, he looked at me expectantly. I guess he was waiting for the same response he always got: 'Whoa man, that's incredible'.

What I actually said was, 'Jarrod, you need help'.

And I didn't mean the 'you need a team' kind of help I'm going to break down in the next chapter. No, I meant he needed someone to rein him in.

Fortunately for Jarrod, this was my speciality.

First, we calculated his EHR. He was making $250,000 a year from this 'side-hustle' of his. Not bad money, right? The thing was, he was working 5,000 hours a year to make it.

Five. Thousand. Hours.

That's an EHR of $50/hour, which seems okay until you realise he was working literally every waking hour.

#nolife

We worked out the EHR of each of Jarrod's offerings. Some of them had a negative EHR and were actually costing him money.

So, how did we 64:4 Jarrod's business?

1. Challenged assumptions

Jarrod felt he needed to keep working as a PE teacher because it gave him credibility with the people he was servicing. I asked him to consider whether he'd have a more positive impact on those people's lives if he got out of the classroom. Getting rid of his teaching job immediately gave him 60 extra hours a week.

Next, I asked Jarrod why he needed to limit the class sizes of his live workshops to 20 people. Those live workshops were his most lucrative product, and by capping the class sizes at 20 he'd put a ceiling on the income he could make from them. To fix this, Jarrod opened up 20 more spots in each workshop. And he sold them all. So he was now making twice as much from his workshops.

Finally, I asked Jarrod why he thought he was the only one who could deliver this live training. Yes, there was a certain amount of expertise only he could bring to the table. But when he hired other experts to deliver his training he realised they had levels of expertise he didn't have. They could give workshop attendees the same positive impact but in a different way.

2. Hit the delete button

We drilled deeper into Jarrod's various offerings and worked out the EHR of each one. Some of them had a negative EHR and were actually costing him money. Getting rid of those products and services was an easy decision to make.

In the end, we got rid of everything except the stuff that was providing the most value—both to Jarrod and to his audience.

3. Amplified the things that worked

Jarrod's live workshops were his best leveraged and best EHR product. How could he amplify their effect?

I've already mentioned one way—delivering them to 40 people at a time rather than 20.

Next, he identified his most highly engaged followers around the world and emailed them to see if they'd be interested in him running a workshop at their school. The result? An all-expenses-paid world tour where he delivered workshops in more than ten countries over six months.

From there, it was an easy jump to run the first ever Connected PE conference.

4. Used proven frameworks

There's a proven framework for pretty much everything out there. I've included several in this book. If you find one that works, by all means, use it. Just make sure you're allowed to use it. (Never steal someone else's work.)

One day, Jarrod decided to copy a sales template I shared in the SuperFastBusiness community. (I'd given permission for others to use it.) And when I say copy, I mean it took him five minutes to change certain elements for his needs and press 'Send'. The result? He immediately secured a $10,000 sponsorship.

When something's worked for other people, there's a good chance it will work for you too.

5. Stopped selling one-time products

It's always hard to leverage selling one-time products. Why? Because you're often selling to a new person every time. (I'll cover this in more detail in Chapters 7 and 8.)

It's been that way for me, Jarrod, and countless others.

But when we combined our products for a given type of customer into a membership where people paid a monthly or yearly subscription, everything changed. It meant we could focus on providing excellent value to our current (and best) customers instead of chasing after new ones.

6. Let go of things he did well

Jarrod was very good at delivering his live workshops. Was he the only one who could deliver his workshops at his level? Yes. Did attendees need someone who could deliver at that level? No.

One thing a lot of business owners struggle with is letting others do the jobs they do well—especially when they enjoy doing them.

But doing those jobs yourself rather than outsourcing them to others stops you from:

Jarrod now uses EHR as a highly effective filter. If it doesn't stack up, he doesn't take it on.

- doing your highest-level work (i.e. the work literally no-one else can do)
- being able to do things like go on holiday and have a life.

Hiring other people to deliver his workshops didn't mean Jarrod *couldn't* deliver them himself. It just meant he didn't *have* to, which gave him freedom to explore other opportunities for his business (and his life).

7. Used EHR as a filter for future projects and opportunities

The craziest thing Jarrod told me was that he was knocking back the chance to deliver live workshops because he didn't have the time.

Those live workshops had an EHR of around $1,500. And yet he was turning them down in favour of work with an EHR of $50 or less.

Jarrod now uses EHR as a highly effective filter. He measures any new opportunity that comes his way against a benchmark of $300/hour. If it doesn't stack up, he doesn't take it on.

Summarising the power of focus and 64:4

Today, Jarrod makes more than half a million dollars a year, and works around 25 hours a week. His current EHR is $380. He has a lot more leisure time at his disposal, and can actually enjoy the money he's making.

Even better, he and his partner have just had a baby and he gets to be highly present in the early months of his first child's life. That's a privilege most new fathers only dream of.

Chapter 3 Action Items

- ❏ Calculate your overall EHR (if you haven't already done so).
- ❏ Calculate the EHR of each of your business activities/products/services.
- ❏ Identify your 4% activities/products/services.
- ❏ Identify the activities/products/services you need to delete.
- ❏ Identify activities you like doing, but could realistically be done by someone else.
- ❏ Identify the EHR you'll use to filter all future opportunities and ideas.
- ❏ Apply that filter to all future opportunities and ideas.

CHAPTER 4
Building a Team

While I was still a general manager and working part-time on my own business, I did everything myself. Mainly because I didn't have a budget for hiring people.

There was no-one around to teach me how this online business worked so I taught myself. As time went on, I developed a sound understanding of the workflows, systems and functions that kept the operations running.

Within a year, however, my business really took off. I needed help managing the workload so I could make better use of my time. Working solo on my own business after coming home from a full-time job was draining.

I started small, hiring someone part-time to help me answer support tickets. By calculating the number of tickets he could answer, and the value of the work I could do as a result, I discovered I'd still make great money after paying his wage.

Next, I recruited the car dealership's part-time receptionist to write content for me. I soon had her writing hundreds of articles for me on a per-article contract. Each one boosted my revenue far more than the cost of hiring her, and she went on to create a thriving content business.

When I quit my job it was time to employ a full-time assistant from the Philippines. I wasn't sure I'd have enough work to keep them busy, but things quickly grew from there and within two years I had more than 60 full-time team members. For the next seven years we supplied online services to hundreds of customers all over the world.

I eventually sold my service businesses, but I still maintain a small but amazing team of highly skilled professionals today. They are mostly based in the Philippines and are vital to me being able to work the hours I want and do the things I want to do most.

If you want to work less and make more, building a strong and functional team is crucial. That's why I'm about to step you through how to set your business up to take on staff. I'll also be sharing my best tips for attracting and retaining great staff, along with the biggest mistakes I've seen people make while trying to build a team.

Getting started

The first step is to get comfortable with the idea of having a team in the first place.

Like a lot of entrepreneurs, you may not enjoy managing people. It may even be why you started your own business in the first place—so you don't have to worry about anyone but yourself. Working on your own without a team runs close to having a job, however.

Having a team frees you up to:

- Do the work you want to do
- Work when you want to
- Generate more profit
- Create an asset you could sell for more money
- Increase the positive impact you have on people in the world (you, your customers, and your team)

The main reason I can work only a few hours each day is that my team magnifies my efforts and does most of the heavy lifting. They do everything I don't need to do and that can't be automated by software.

A team is also key to scaling your business so it can make more money. The clients I coach are usually the biggest bottleneck in their own businesses. But once they create systems and processes for everything they do and hand them off to someone else, those bottlenecks disappear.

Looking at all those tasks on your wall, you'll notice some you don't actually need to do. They take up time and add no value to your business.

And they're not scared to take on more work because they know the team can handle it.

Before you start building a team, however, you need to do four things:

Exercise 1: Delete

Every time you perform a business task you need to do more than once, write it on a Post-it note.

Yes, every single one.

Do it for a month, and then put all those Post-it notes on a wall in your office or study.

Looking at all those tasks on your wall, you'll notice some you don't actually need to do. **They take up time and add no value to your business.**

Now put the Post-it notes for those tasks in the bin, and never do them again. (If you're worried you might, create a to-don't list as a reminder.)

Exercise 2: Delegate

Next, you need to figure out what can be delegated. They may be things you hate doing, or can be done better by someone else.

The hardest tasks to let go are the ones you enjoy doing— researching, choosing stock images, editing media, or fiddling with fonts on your website. These are low-return tasks other people can do. You need to let go of them so you have more time for the stuff only you can do.

Put these tasks in a 'Delegate' pile. We'll deal with them soon.

Exercise 3: Do

Once you've figured out what can be deleted and delegated, you should be left with only the absolute highest-level activities that are both important and urgent.

And that's the ultimate goal of building a team—to ensure you do only those high-level, high-impact tasks, and then build a routine around them.

Exercise 4: Detail

See all those tasks on Post-it notes in the 'Delegate' pile? Whenever you tackle one over the next month, write down or record how you do it. (The steps should be easy enough for a school kid to follow.) Once you've documented the steps for doing something, you'll never have to do it again because someone else can.

That someone can be your mum, your kid, or a Virtual Assistant (VA). It doesn't matter who it is as long as they're reliable, and don't charge as much for their time as you do for yours.

This is where EHR is a great filter. If you can pay someone less than your current EHR to do something, you should. The higher your EHR, the more you'll be able to pay other people to do these tasks in your business.

How to attract and retain great staff

Whether your team members are in your office, the next suburb or the Philippines, managing people can be a challenge. But while processes can ease this, you must avoid processing people.

Instead, you need to measure *results and progress*.

And as soon as you trust your staff, lift the restrictions. Asking what they're up to every five minutes and demanding screen shares to prove they're working is humiliating and demotivating. You wouldn't like it, and neither will your team members.

Give them free reign and, providing you've hired the right people, you'll be amazed at what they can do.

Here are my best tips for attracting and retaining great staff:

1. Use filters and checklists

At Mercedes-Benz I created a checklist for recruiting new salespeople. It was important that whoever I was interviewing met the criteria for that role. If they got all ticks, I hired them. If they didn't, I let them know they weren't a good fit for us.

The best time to fire someone is before you hire them. Having a filtering checklist sorted before you hire will make your life a lot easier. You'll also be able to hire people

To a certain
extent your team
is there to make
you redundant.

faster than other businesses, which will give you the best choice of candidates.

2. Down tools and manage

Once you've hired people to do your tasks, make sure you stop doing them yourself. I've seen businesses languish because the owner can't leave the coalface long enough to think, rest, plan, innovate or even lead. It frustrates and demotivates the person hired to do the job, and cancels out the benefit of having staff in the first place.

To a certain extent your team is there to make you redundant which, as I'll soon cover, is a major survival strategy for running your own business.

3. Establish, document and communicate procedures for everything

Creating Standard Operating Procedures (SOPs) is an essential part of handing tasks over to another person. It also makes assessing performance and replicating success much easier. You're essentially creating your business's DNA so it can survive beyond your current team. Your library of SOPs should be centrally located (online is good) so you can easily share them with whoever's doing each task.

And make sure you keep a copy.

4. Communicate your expectations and monitor performance

If you have a team (even if that team is just you and another person), share your vision and financial goals for the business.

Set goals for them that feed into that vision, and then regularly check in with them on how they're progressing and performing.

Many sales-based professions have a 100% churn rate every year. Why? Because no-one pulls them up for poor form in the early stages of their job or asks, 'What can we do to help you?'

5. Reward the behaviour you want

Many leaders spend their time looking for what's wrong. Instead of focusing all your attention on what your staff 'mess up' or need to change, look for what they're doing right. Reward and reinforce the behaviour you want. *The One Minute Manager* covers this well, and is a valuable resource if you're new to managing people.

6. Conduct regular tune-ups

When I was at the dealership I'd run a daily 'reset' for my team.

First thing in the morning we'd get together and discuss what everyone was working on that day and take notes on a whiteboard. This quick stand-up meeting:

1. Eliminated overlap

2. Reduced miscommunication

3. Renewed focus

4. Provided a forum for company news announcements (e.g. 'We're getting a-load of new key rings today and will be using them from tomorrow')

5. Identified areas where people needed help.

It inspired me to run similar meetings in my own business—daily until we had everything dialled in, and then weekly.

We now spend just 12 minutes in our weekly tune-up, but our team communication is high. I often ask team members to run the meeting so they feel part of the business. They like the work they're doing and are keen to communicate with their colleagues. Because they all work remotely it's a great way for them to connect, and to reinforce our social culture. We also use an online collaboration tool between tune-ups to stay connected.

7. Establish the values of your business with your team

In my business, our values are: integrity, communication, confidentiality and high-level skills. We embrace discretion because for the most part we operate under the radar. Our focus is the customer and the results we get for them. There's no ego in my business.

*People with an
entrepreneurial mindset
can wear different hats
and tackle problems
creatively.*

What does your business stand for, and how does your team contribute to it? Your team values should be formed by the team and then used for hiring, training and tune-ups.

8. Encourage Involvement

Be clear on the results you want, and consult with your staff on how you as a team will get there. When I go to Manila to spend time with my team, I let them know where the business is at, and what my overarching goal is. I then invite them to talk about how we can get there. When they're providing the drive and ideas that will help the business achieve its goals, they're more invested in the process and everyone benefits.

9. Don't hire employees

Having a team of people with an employee mindset means you have to cater for employees. But people with an entrepreneurial mindset can wear different hats and tackle problems creatively. They will help you run your business instead of just doing whatever they're told so they can get their paycheque.

I suggest screening out anyone who shows signs of dependency. It may sound harsh, but you'll end up with a far more motivated, productive workforce and better results.

The four biggest mistakes people make when building a team

I've invested 20 years into hiring and firing experiences, and the better part of five years coaching people on building their own teams. Here are four mistakes I see businesses make over and over.

Mistake #1: Slow to hire

If you genuinely don't have the money to hire anyone, it means you don't have good cash flow and/or an offer that converts. If that's the case, then you need to implement what you'll be learning in Chapters 5 and 6.

If you *do* have good cash flow and an offer that converts, then you can afford to hire someone. You just need to get past the mindset that you can't. I've had so many students hire people on my say-so and then come back to me and say, 'I wish I'd done this sooner'. It's gratifying, but also a little frustrating.

The other mindset you need to let go of is the idea of *selling time*.

When you hire someone, you shift your mindset to one of *buying time*. Happily, plenty of people are willing to sell us their time as a job. As entrepreneurs, we get to package up and re-sell their time.

My great grandfather used to buy plots of land in Russia and sell them in America. He had gold and silver mines in Australia, Japan and Malaysia. He took advantage of geographic arbitrage to buy low and sell high.

You can do this right now. The current hot spot is the Philippines. Labour is their number one export, and they have great English.

Mistake #2: No systems

The second big mistake people make is not having systems. If you don't have systems, then you don't have a business. Why not? Because you don't have anything you can sell. You're just freewheeling it.

Here are some of the core systems I have in my business:

ASSET REGISTER

The most important document we have in our business is our asset register. It's the DNA that holds everything together.

An asset register is an easily accessible document that lists all the important things in your business such as:

- Domain name and hosting access
- The team's SOPs
- Your stock library of images, logos and media
- And so on.

It's important that at least two people can do every task in your business. I call this the Noah Principle.

NOAH PRINCIPLE

If a task can only be done by one person, and that person wants to leave, then you may have to either:

- Take over, and do the task yourself
- Give them a huge pay rise to convince them to stay.

This illustrates both single point sensitivity and compromise, which can create a lot of drama for your business. Your EHR will go down, and your stress levels will go up.

That's why it's important that at least two people can do every task in your business. I call this the Noah Principle. It protects you, and removes unnecessary compromises from your business operations. If someone leaves, your team member can hire and train a replacement while you get on with the high-impact tasks.

SMALL BATCHES

A friend of mine created a new course, and his assistant edited 27 videos for it. Later, he found out they'd added a royalty-protected Justin Bieber backing track to them. 'Hey, this is great,' my friend says to his team member. 'But we can't use that music. So, please redo all the videos.'

Re-doing those videos took six weeks.

This is the equivalent of painting a whole house before checking the colour on a test wall.

Encourage your team to do the smallest possible job sample first, and then show you the result. Once you've checked it and approved it, they can do the whole batch.

CROSS CHECK

If you've ever flown, then you've probably heard the phrase, 'Cabin crew, cross check doors'.

Our eyes often see what should be there instead of what's actually there, which is how errors slip through. Your team members shouldn't be checking their own work. If someone writes an email or publishes a website page—anything client-facing—someone else with fresh eyes should check it *before* it goes out. In our business the simple rule is, 'You cannot check your own work'.

STANDARD OPERATING PROCEDURES (SOPS)

As mentioned earlier, SOPs are instructions so clear a 14-year-old kid could follow them without any prior knowledge.

Everything in your business that happens more than once should have an SOP. It should be shared with everyone who does that role, and updated regularly.

Our SOPs are just simple docs linked from our Asset Register.

RULES FOR TOOLS

If you look at your credit card statement, you'll probably see monthly subscriptions for a host of online tools. They cost a lot of money, but how many of them do you actually use?

For this reason, any tool we use in our business must meet the following criteria:

1. **Required.** It must be essential to the operations of our business. If it's not, it's out and we delete it.

2. **Know how to use it.** At least two people in our team must be fluent in it. They must have also done all the training and tested out the support.

3. **Best of breed.** It's got to be the best tool for the job. If it's no longer the best, we switch to something else.

SIMPLE PROJECT MANAGEMENT

We've tried Trello, Asana, Teamwork, Basecamp and more. And you know what we're currently using? Google Docs, Google Sheets and Google Drive. That's it. For $35 a month.

As far as visually representing where projects are at, we use the same system Toyota used to manufacture cars: *Kanban*. This is a three-column system of:

- To do
- Doing
- Done

It's great if two people know how to do something. It's even better if three people know.

This allows us to get a very quick read on:

- What projects do we have on?
- Which ones haven't we started?
- Which ones have we finished?

PODS OF THREE

Amazon's Jeff Bezos talks about teams being small enough to feed with one pizza. I've found pods of three are great. Why three? Well, you can cross-train with three people. It's great if two people know how to do something. It's even better if three people know.

Another advantage of having three people in a team is that someone's going to step up. How do you know who'll step up? Have a meeting and say, 'I'm going to hand it over to you. Can someone lead the meeting?' After a pause, someone will pipe up with, 'I'll do it, boss'. There's your team leader. Now train them to look after the other two. If the team leader is away, the other two will step in and take over.

This is especially good because it allows people to have leave and recharge.

I have a team for research and development, and one for content. What do you do when you need another pod? Take one from the team of three and say, 'You're now the team leader in your own team of three'.

Mistake #3: No training

Let's take a quick trip back to 1995.

It was the end of my first day at BMW, and by the time I finished it was getting dark. I went to the key board so I could drive a car home, and the only key left was for a Boston Green 316i manual.

I went out to the nature strip where the car was. All the chains and boards were up, and everyone else had driven away. It was just me, this car, and the darkness.

I opened the car and, after some time, figured out where to put the key. (It was in a weird spot.) But I couldn't figure out how to turn the lights on. Instead of being on the indicator stalk like every other car, it was on the dash, hidden somewhere in the pitch black.

I won't tell you how long it took me to turn the lights on because it's too embarrassing. But when I did, I discovered the car had no petrol. Great.

I went to a petrol station, put fuel in the car, got a receipt, and came back the next day.

The dealership refused to reimburse me because I was supposed to use their on-site fuel bowser. Something no-one had told me.

That evening, the whole rigmarole started again. At the end of the day I rushed to the key board, and once again the only car left was the Boston Green 316i manual. I was destined to become friends with this car.

But this time my work associate Elden was there, swinging the keys to a 7 Series.

'James, you're new here,' he said. 'Would you like to swap cars with me? You try the 7 Series.'

'Are you sure?'

'Yeah. Here you go.'

At the last second he jerked the keys away from me and said, 'Suck my dick!' before sliding into the 7 Series and purring off into the dark.

I drove the 316i home a bit offended and somewhat confused.

What's my point here? I didn't get any training at all. On my first day they pointed me to a desk, and that was literally it.

Now, let's fast-forward to 1999.

Two years after selling the most BMWs in Australia within a year of starting, I switched to Mercedes-Benz. After two years I was their top-selling salesperson, and was promoted to sales manager. When that happened, I got a little team: two salespeople and a rookie sales cadet.

By 2001 my salespeople were winning every sales competition. I won Sales Manager of the Year, and Mercedes-Benz said, 'We need you to tell the other sales managers what you're doing.'

What was my secret? It was so simple.

*A decade later, many of
the people I'd trained
were running dealerships
in Australia. I'm quite
proud of this.*

THE STARTER PACK

When someone came in on their first day, I gave them a starter pack containing everything they needed to do their job.

They got a notebook, an employment agreement, a name badge, and a form to tell us which bank account their pay should go into. They got a rundown of where everything was and what they needed to do. I was adamant no-one would ever experience the confusion I felt when I started at BMW.

I also talked to them about their goals. I asked them why they were there, and what they wanted to achieve.

Finally, I talked to them about the culture. What does it mean to work at this business? Who are we? Where do we come from? Why is it called Mercedes-Benz? When was it founded? What's the history?

I made them feel genuinely welcome. I got them excited about their new role, and set the tone for things going forward.

Here are a few other training-related principles I brought to the table:

COMPETENCY-BASED TRAINING

The best course I ever went on was a motorcycle course.

They started by making us walk the motorcycle around the yard. If we mastered that, we could sit on the bike.

If we mastered that, we could turn on the ignition. If we mastered that, we could start it. And if we mastered that, we could put it into gear and pull the clutch in.

That's how I ran my training. Here's what I said to my new staff:

> *It takes as long as it takes. You don't go to the next item until you've ticked the box on the item before it. When you have a tick in every box on this page, you can sell cars. Until then, you can't. Let's start now.*

In my training system, people needed to investigate, plan, be persistent, be organised, do teamwork, be punctual, take notes, and have self-discipline and urgency—all attributes of a great sales professional. If they passed my training, I knew they'd be great salespeople.

And they were.

A decade later, many of the people I'd trained were running dealerships in Australia. I'm quite proud of this.

TREAT THEM LIKE A CUSTOMER

On their first day, I'd take each salesperson down to their car, which would be beautifully washed and cleaned, and full of fuel. (A bit different to my first experience.) And I'd give them a complete tour of the car as if they were buying it.

They'd drive home in this car. And then they'd open an envelope I'd given them and read my questionnaire that asked things like:

Okay, you just drove home in a brand-new Mercedes-Benz. How did it feel? Did you notice other people looking at you? What did you notice about the way the car drives?

Next morning, they'd come in and tell me:

I felt special. People made way for me. They were too scared to run into me. The car was quiet yet powerful, and handled really well.

To which I'd say:

Retain that feeling of the first time you drove a brand-new Mercedes-Benz. Because that's what prospects will experience on their test drive.

Get your team to feel what you want your customers to feel. It will do wonders for your business. (And in case you're wondering, I coach my team the same way I coach my clients.)

EARLY DETECTION

I could tell whether or not someone would be a good salesperson even before they finished their competency-based training. The best people got through the training within a week. If someone was still training after two weeks, I'd politely suggest they weren't a good fit.

Let them grow instead.
Let them stretch a bit.
Let them struggle so they
get stronger.

NO SPOON-FEEDING

It's so tempting to spoon-feed new people in your business. But let them grow instead. Let them stretch a bit. Let them struggle so they get stronger.

And have them refer to their notes. Whenever they ask about something you know you've covered or they've been trained on, say, 'Go back to your notes and check. If you still can't find it, ask me again'.

DO YOU HAVE TO KNOW HOW TO DO SOMETHING TO TRAIN SOMEONE?

No, you don't. As my friend Dean Jackson says, 'You don't need to know how, you need to know who'. I don't know anything about Facebook advertising. If I want someone in my team to run Facebook ads, I'd send them to a masterclass. I sent the person who does my Facebook advertising to a $5,000 workshop in the USA. It was worth it.

TEACH YOUR TEAM ABOUT THE POWER OF 64:4

Having read Chapter 3, you know that not all tasks are created equal. Do your team members know this? Unless you've specifically discussed it with them, they probably don't.

If my webmaster is thinking, 'Should I do the sales offer page James requested, or update the WordPress installation on our fourth most important podcast site?', which one do you think she should do?

Obviously the sales offer page is far more important.

Show your team how to think, and how to distinguish between tasks. You don't have to go all micro on them. Just ensure they understand the result you're shooting for as a team, and which tasks will help you achieve them the fastest.

BOUNCE POORLY DONE TASKS

The first time you get a job back, it may not meet your standards. Avoid doing the praise-feedback-praise thing: 'Oh look, you made a good effort. It's not quite good enough, but you did try hard.' That's called a shit sandwich. And it doesn't taste good.

Just say, 'Here's the example we had. And here's where I feel it hasn't met the standard. Let's redo it.'

Plain, simple language. Nothing tricky.

The problem with the positive-negative-positive is you put the positive out there and they're like 'Aahhh'. Then you kick them in the guts and they're like 'Oohh'. And then you bring them up again.

It's very confusing for people, and they never know when to trust you.

Be straight with them so that when you praise them for doing good work it's real praise.

Mistake #4: Poor leadership

'To err is human'—Alexander Pope.

When you have a team, the business train is going to run off the tracks at some point.

Your job as a leader is to put the train back on the tracks when it derails. Don't get frustrated about the fact it's come off, or take it as a sign that having a team is a bad idea. Remember, having a team means you don't have to spend your days driving the train.

Here are some thoughts about being the leader your team needs:

LEAVE THE BUSINESS EVERY SO OFTEN

These days I judge my business's success on whether or not I can leave my laptop behind when I go on holiday. True success isn't being at the beach with your laptop. It's being at the beach without your laptop.

I learn a lot about my business when I go on holiday, because when I come back I discover:

- What broke
- Who stepped up
- Who took initiative
- Who created something amazing
- What should have been done but didn't get done (and where the gaps are)

Any system that caters for the lowest common denominator pulls down the high performers.

- Who isn't cross-trained
- Which system failed
- The results we got

I help my team improve these things and fill the gaps, which means a stronger system while I'm around *and* the next time I go away.

GIVE YOUR BEST TO YOUR BEST

A huge mistake I see people making a lot is focusing on the squeaky wheels in their team and creating systems for them.

Any system that caters for the lowest common denominator pulls down the high performers.

As a high performer in my previous roles, I resented anything designed for the average person, which included all sorts of constraints and reporting requirements.

If someone needs these constraints and reporting to perform well for you, send them on their way. They're holding your business back.

ZOOM IN AND OUT

Micromanaging sucks.

Be present at times, but also be willing to offer some space. Zoom in and out.

Choose the items you zoom in on carefully. While some people track their employees' time to make sure they're not on Facebook, doing their banking online or whatever, I already know they're on Facebook (like every other adult).

I'll zoom in on our daily numbers and talk about the results we're achieving (traffic, leads, conversions) and then I'll zoom out.

I want a high-impact result, and I'm happy to get one report at the start of the day: What are you doing today?

And at the end of the day: What did you achieve today?

That's it.

BE SELF-AWARE

I once had a boss that made Darth Vader look like a nice guy.

Here's an example of just how nuts he was.

One day he noticed a tiny speck of dust on the front driveway of our dealership. After demanding a broom from the mechanic, he snatched it from him and started furiously sweeping the small pile of dirt to the kerb. But the dirt wouldn't cooperate with his sweeping action, making him angrier and angrier. In the end he slammed the broomstick into a customer's car, denting the panel. The car had to be taken to a repair shop to be painted and returned the next day.

If he saw a Coca-Cola can on a salesperson's desk he'd karate chop it across the showroom.

Over time, the staff were so scared of him they avoided him. And the more the staff respected me, the more it got under his skin.

One day, after drinking several quadruple Sambucas, he accused me of having 'too much talent', then spat on my shoe and told me to get another job.

The beauty of a bad boss is they show you what not to do.

But, what if you're the bad boss?

I see it happen sometimes. The more successful and CEO people get, the more of a tyrant they become. They get a bit too full of themselves, and start taking on some undesirable characteristics—a slight air of belligerence and thinking they're different. They make no time for the team, and understandably the team starts looking elsewhere.

When I was teaching a new person how to sell cars, I'd occasionally take off my cufflinks, roll up my sleeves and wash the car with them. I wanted them to know I didn't expect them to do anything I wasn't willing to do myself.

If you're seeing 'bad boss' behaviour in yourself, the fastest way to arrest it is to get back to the coalface for a second. Get a dose of humility, and connect with a fellow human.

*If people are rolling
out every month or two,
chances are you're not
a good boss.*

Getting the best results from your team

Here are a few more ninja tips for nurturing a team and ensuring you're getting the most out of them.

Watch for staff turnover

The newest person in my team started six years ago. Some of my team members have been with me for eight years. And in that time a lot of them have become very close, personal friends. We have great relationships, and I visit them regularly.

That's a huge factor. If your team is remote, make the effort to visit your team or have them visit you.

But if people are rolling out every month or two, chances are you're not a good boss. They're probably leaving you, not the job.

In this situation, it's important to conduct exit interviews. You'll get some of the most honest feedback you'll ever have about what you're like as a boss. Be prepared to take suggestions on how you can improve.

Traffic light report

If you ask your team to sprint every day, you'll wear them out. They'll blow up and disappoint you. Even worse, if your team is burnt out they won't serve your customers very well.

Top athletes value rest.

At the end of each day I ask every team member to send me a little report, and to tell me whether they're red, yellow or green.

If they're green, I know I can load them up.

Yellow means they're having high impact, and are approaching the limit of their capacity.

If they're red, I know they're running a bit hot. At which point I dial things back so I don't overcook them.

Share your reporting

In our business we look at only a few numbers. And every day we share those numbers with the entire team.

The numbers give everyone an idea of how healthy the business is. As they know a healthy business means a secure and fun job, the team is heavily invested in those numbers.

Keep your team in the loop, and you'll be surprised at how much ownership they'll take of your business' success.

Everyone in the team can influence those numbers. They're not financial figures, but rather lead metrics such as website visits, number of subscribers, and emails we've sent in the past 30 days.

We compare yesterday to last month to six months ago. No fancy dashboards—just a screenshot of a spreadsheet.

Oh, and the numbers are put there by a team member, not me.

Have an infinity project

People often hesitate about hiring someone because they're not sure there will be enough work to keep them busy. That's why it's good to have an infinity project.

When I sold a few of my businesses, I started thinking about creating a new business. And I thought, 'You know what? I want to create new business we can sell in the future'.

Our new project now has a lot of traffic and subscribers. It's our infinity project—what the team works on when we don't have any high-impact work to do.

If my team is reporting green, I know they'll be spending time over there.

There's no limit on how many blog posts they can write for that site. We have a news feed pouring articles into our team hub. My team looks through them, picks the best ones, researches them, and then schedules posts for the following week. I know the wages I'm spending on my full-time team is helping me build an asset I can sell one day. They also have a cool 'skunkworks' project where they can learn, experiment and have fun outside of our core business.

Keep your team in the loop, and you'll be surprised at how much ownership they'll take of your business' success.

Celebrate lack of drama

If you do all of these things, you'll get to a more peaceful place. You'll experience less overload. Other people will do the things that need to happen in your business instead of you. You can go to a conference and not worry about your business stopping dead in its tracks. You're now selling other people's results and/or time instead of yours.

And you're probably well on your way to creating a business you might be able to sell one day.

In the meantime, you have a business where you can make more while working less.

Chapter 4 Action Items

- ☐ Perform the delete-delegate-do exercise at the beginning of the chapter.
- ☐ Start writing SOPs for every task that's done more than once in your business.
- ☐ Create an asset register.
- ☐ If you currently have a team, ask yourself:
    - ☐ Are there any team members that should be moved on because they're holding back your business?
    - ☐ Are there any team members who can handle more responsibility?

MORE READING/LISTENING

Visit JamesSchramko.com for a secret bonus chapter plus a list of recommended resources and additional notes that expand on this topic.

CHAPTER 5
An Offer that Converts

In 2007 I was General Manager of a Mercedes-Benz dealership, and probably making more than any other GM in the country.

But I was tired of the motor trade. I wanted to be the one buying Mercedes-Benz AMGs, not selling them.

You'll recall I was also hyper-aware of my single-point sensitivity. A financial crisis was looming in the USA. If it dragged Australia down with it, I could have ended up in the same position my father was all those years ago—redundant, living in an expensive city with a family and a mortgage to support, and unable to replace the salary of a high-paying job.

My best customers were successful business owners, and so the path was clear: *I needed my own successful business.*

Which is why I spent every single night between 9.30pm and 3am in my living room trying to build one.

In the end, it took me nine months to make my first dollar online. Why? Because that's how long it took me to find an *offer that converts.*

What is an offer that converts?

In short, it's when:

1. You give people the opportunity to buy something from you (the offer)
2. They buy it (it converts).

If you send an email to someone saying, 'For $150 I can come to your house and tell you which trees to plant in your backyard,' and they respond with, 'Sounds good, see you Tuesday,' you have an offer that converts.

If you have a book up on Amazon that's selling three copies a day, that's an offer that converts.

If you hand-paint rocks and people buy them from you at a local market on Sundays, you have an offer that converts.

What if you don't have an offer that converts?

Then you can't make an income.

And you can't expect to have a flexible lifestyle, an online business or a way to quit your job if you don't have an income.

It's like a farmer expecting to harvest a crop without planting any seeds.

Time and again I see people register a new business. They immediately get someone to design a logo, print business cards and build a website, thinking these are the most important things to do first.

Wrong.

The most the important thing to do first is to offer something and have people pay you for it. Once you have an offer that converts, then you have the makings of a viable business.

The first website I actually made money with was as ugly as hell. There was no logo or even a business name. Just an offer.

I was selling website building software and collecting an affiliate commission for every sale.

With that website, I ended up making my first $100,000 as a business owner.

Someone else I know started a successful business without a business name, logo or website. All she had was a Google sheet for people to fill out. When they were ready to buy, she sent them to a payment button and they made their purchase. From there, she communicated with them via email and Skype.

Why am I telling you this?

*When you have offer
and conversion, you
have income. Now
you're in business.*

To prove you don't need to invest a lot of time and money upfront to build a successful and profitable business.

You don't need a lot of tech.

You don't even need a business name.

You just need to follow two steps:

Step 1: Offer something people can buy right now

It's amazing how many new business owners fail to do this. Perhaps the dream of having a business is enough for them to talk about on social media and at dinner parties.

But they're not making an offer. And that's a problem, because if they're not making an offer, they can't make a sale. And remember: no sale = no income.

Let's assume you're not one of those people. Let's assume you are making an offer. Are people buying? Because that's a key part of this step—conversion.

When you have offer and conversion, you have income. Now you're in business and can do the next step.

Step 2: Scale it

'Scale it' simply means 'do more of it'.

That's all I did with that first website I made money from. I found a way to generate income by offering website-building software to people who were struggling to build a website. Once I had buyers, I directed all my energy into making that offer to more and more people until it became a six-figure-per-year income stream.

There are exceptions, of course, but if you can't scale your offer it's going to be difficult to build a long-term, viable business from it.

Some traps to avoid

I've been coaching clients for more than ten years, and in that time, I've seen people making the same mistakes over and over. Let's see if I can help you avoid making them with your offer.

1. Not every idea is a good one

People often say, 'I've got a great idea. Please help me take it to market and sell it. Let's see if we can find some customers to buy it'.

This is a difficult way to go about things.

If you're an entrepreneur and you're creative, you'll come up with a zillion ideas. But before you pursue those ideas you should validate them (see next point).

2. The difference between preference and performance

People often say they'll do something (preference), but don't follow through (performance).

It's a big problem for business owners, and the reason I tend not to build something unless people pay for it first.

Now, you might think, 'That's insane. How does that even work? Do people really pay for something before you make it?'

Yes. And here's an example.

For my annual live event, I put up the event sales offer page and drive people to it from my email database. I usually sell around 100 tickets in the first 24 hours. That's performance. Now I'm comfortable paying the venue and confirming my booking for the event.

If it turned out I couldn't sell the event, or people said, 'Sorry, I can't come because I'm busy/overseas/going to see Richard Branson and Tony Robbins', then I might change my plans.

This is why you shouldn't build *anything* to any great depth before you validate it (i.e. ask people to pay for it).

3. Reluctance sabotage

Some people avoid the possibility of rejection by never actually making an offer. I think it stems back to the caveman era, where being rejected by your tribe meant you were probably going to die.

The fun thing is, there's no real downside today if someone says no. In fact, it's inevitable it will happen. High-converting sales pages might convert at five or even ten percent, but never 100 percent.

The faster you can progress an idea and test it, the faster you can decide whether to pursue it or dump it.

There will always be people who say no to your offer.

As soon as you get comfortable with that reality, and understand that you can't have a 'Yes' without a 'No', the core reluctance disappears. Take the yesses and prosper.

4. Perfectionism

Trying to get all your ducks in a row and make everything perfect will torture you. In most cases, reasonable is fine so just go with a 'good enough' first draft.

The beauty of the online world, in particular, is it's so easy to change things. If you find out something isn't working, you can easily make the necessary tweaks.

The fastest way to progress ideas

You probably have a notebook (or Evernote file) full of ideas. They're coming to you from other people in the form of joint ventures. They arrive in your inbox from people asking questions. They come out of every conversation you have with clients.

The faster you can progress an idea and test it, the faster you can decide whether to pursue it or dump it. Here are two ways to progress ideas:

1. Operate at low resolution rather than high definition

What's the minimum version of your idea? The smallest, simplest version?

When I'm coaching, people often come to me with enormous mind maps they've spent years researching, scheming and perfecting.

'Here's what I'm going to do,' they say.

It's easy to get caught in analysis paralysis—the mode where you keep adding, refining and modifying without ever getting to the next stage. Your once simple hand-drawn notes end up looking like the wiring diagram of a NASA spacecraft.

That's why I respond with, 'Whoa! Okay, let's put a circle around that first node on your massive mind map. Let's do just that'.

Going back to my first venture, the smallest version I started with was, *Can I find someone struggling to build a website, and sell them software that makes that job easy?*

That was it. My first $100,000 of online income came from just one product, and it wasn't even mine. I was just an affiliate for it.

How's that for a simple, low-resolution idea?

2. Go low tech

I've already mentioned my friend who doesn't have a business card, business name, website or fancy sales page.

You don't need them at the moment either. You just need human contact.

While watching my kids play soccer, I'd talk to other mums and dads about online marketing, and how interesting it was. I'd show them things on my phone, and send them my affiliate links if they were interested in building their own website.

When you keep things low tech, you reduce your investment (i.e. time and money) in the idea. This means you can quickly test ideas, and move on from the bad ones.

Filtering ideas

Of course, the hardest thing about having all these ideas is deciding which ones to progress. Here are some of my favourite filters:

1. What's the EHR?

This is the best filter to try first on any idea.

Let's say you're an expert at something, and you're thinking of offering a coaching service. If a client pays you $1,000 a month and you spend ten hours a month servicing them, that's an EHR of $100. The client paying $5,000 a month

You can't filter on EHR alone. You should also look at whether your idea can scale.

might seem better until you realise you'll be spending 100 hours a month servicing them, which gives an EHR of only $50.

2. Can it scale?

You can't filter on EHR alone. You should also look at whether your idea can scale.

Let's go back to our coaching example where you're charging $1,000 a month and spending ten hours per person.

In any given month, you can dedicate around 180 hours to your business. If you spend 80 of them organising yourself and doing what it takes to run a business, you only have 100 hours left. Which means you can only ever service ten clients each month.

Ten clients paying $1,000 each month comes to $10,000 a month, or $120,000 dollars a year.

But you can't scale it, so your annual income is capped at $120,000.

To increase your income, you'd need to change your offer. That could mean:

- Coaching one-to-many instead of one-to-one
- Charging more
- Spending fewer hours with each client

Now you can see why EHR is such a great tool, especially when combined with scale.

3. Does it offer recurring income?

Can we make it a recurring offer? My best offers are evergreen—the income never stops. Once the hard work of the sale is done, you keep getting paid over and over again. (I'll talk about this more in Chapter 8.)

4. Can I sell it later?

Are you building something you can sell? I avoid building businesses around my personal brand. I want to make sure I'm always in a position to sell.

5. Is the market growing?

I prefer growing markets. Look for emerging popularity. What are people optimistic about, starting to use more, or excited about? Be wary of going into a declining market. The bottom might fall out of it just as you get your idea going. What a waste of time and effort.

6. Is there demand?

Yesterday a customer asked me if they should invest $50,000 in a project they're considering. My first question was, 'Who's already in this market selling this stuff?'

They found a company doing somewhere between two to five million dollars a year in the same market with almost the same product. That made me a lot more comfortable about the business. If people were already selling and, most importantly, buying the product, there was a market for it.

Advertising is another good indicator. Are there ads out there for what you're selling? If there are Google searches for the product or service, there's a good chance people are buying.

7. Can you access the customers?

In some markets, customers 'cost' a lot more. For example, you'd pay a lot more for a prospect in the legal market than you would in the sporting market where you could get more volume at lower rates. It's harder to get yourself in front of Fortune 500 CEOs than it is to get in front of parents.

Before chasing an idea, make sure the barriers between you and the market are absent, or at least surmountable.

8. Does it fit a passion?

There's a time for eating beans and crawling over broken glass. In other words, doing things you don't love.

I've lugged wet timber out of cargo containers. I've dug holes with a shovel. I've driven around collecting money from late payers. I've done all sorts of jobs that weren't high on my passion meter because I had kids to feed and bills to pay.

That's why I love the fact that now, a decade after starting my own business, I'm in a position where I can work on things I want to work on.

*Don't pursue ideas
just because they can
make money.*

If you're in the same position, passion is an important filter. Don't pursue ideas just because they can make money.

9. Will the customer be better off?

What's the most recent thing you purchased? Whether it was food, fuel or business coaching from SuperFastBusiness, you bought it because you wanted to be better off.

If your product or service can make people better off, it's a good idea.

Before putting together your offer

Once you've narrowed down your list of ideas and decided which offer to make, it's time to make it. But first you need to be able to answer these questions:

1. Who is your customer?

What's their age, gender, household income, family status? What are their problems?

2. What is your actual offer?

What problem will you solve for the customer?

3. Who are you?

Why should the customer choose you to solve their problem?

4. How much is it?

What are you charging the customer to solve their problem?

Pricing your offer

One of the most vexing questions is how to price an offer. It depends on the market, your industry, and you. Here are some things to consider:

1. Comparison

This is most useful when you have a current reference point. For example, if you're selling TVs, you could walk around a store or go online and see what other TVs cost. Do your research as if you were buying your own product. What choices do you have?

If you're coming into this kind of market, one strategy might be to find the top three choices in the market. You can then come in at a premium price that implies you're the best. (You'd need something to back that up.) Or you might come in cheap in a race-to-the-bottom-type market you're trying to undercut. (This is always a difficult game, and I generally advise against it because Amazon will beat you.)

Slotting in at a similar price point is another approach. If you do this, make sure you have something to differentiate your offer from those of your competitors.

2. Cost plus margin

This is where you work out what something costs you, add a margin (it should be quite a lot), and come up with a price.

Let's say I know a brilliant artist who designs t-shirts, and they charge me $20 to customise a t-shirt. I might think, *I need to make $50 for every t-shirt I sell, so I'm going to sell these beautiful, custom-made t-shirts for $70.* That's a cost-plus-margin deal.

Other costs will be coming out of your revenue—staff, advertising, logistics, rent, electricity, design, etc. You need plenty of margin to cover them.

You'd be surprised how many businesses have higher costs than what they sell their products and services for. And when they add them all up at the end of the year, they discover they've made a loss.

Don't be one of those businesses. The easiest way to make a profit is to earn more than you spend.

3. Value to client

This is a good one, especially in coaching. I offer six months of coaching for $10,000. Someone considering my offer is already making $200,000 a year. So I'm suggesting they invest five percent of their profit to help generate far more than the $10,000 they're spending.

It doesn't matter how amazing your offer is. If you can't grab your market's attention, they'll never find out about it.

The reality is I can do that easily—usually within a few months. It's a smart investment, and an easy choice to make. That's why the conversions are ultra-high.

4. Make it up

If you can't find anyone else in your category, or you can't decide on a price, just choose one and go with it. It's better than not making an offer at all. See if anyone buys it at that price. You can always change it later.

Communicating your offer

Okay, so you know what your offer is, and you know the price. Now it's time to let everyone know about it. Here are the five key elements you might consider when doing this:

1. Strong headline

It doesn't matter how amazing your offer is. If you can't grab your market's attention, they'll never find out about it and you won't make any sales.

2. Address the problem

What pain is the customer experiencing? What are their challenges? What's stopping them from being successful? What are they struggling with? What keeps them up at night? What problem are they desperately trying to solve?

3. Address the implications of not solving the problem

Remember, people buy to be better off.

So what will happen if they don't buy what you're offering? Will their problems get worse? Will they miss out on something? Will their life stay the same?

4. Make a relevant and results-based promise

You know who the customer is. You know their pain points. And you have something that addresses that pain.

Now's the time to promise what your offer delivers. Ideally, you should tell your customers what results they'll get, and how quickly they'll get them.

For example: 'Increase your email list by 500 subscribers in 30 days.'

How do you know if your promise is relevant? It has to pass the 'So what?' test. If you make an offer to your ideal customer and they say, 'So what?', your offer needs refining.

5. Tell them how to buy

This is important. Tell them very clearly how to buy what you're offering.

'On the next page, you'll see the checkout. Simply fill it in and make your purchase.'

By spelling things out, you'll get more conversions.

Enhancing your offer

The five elements I just mentioned are the minimum boxes you need to tick when telling everyone about your offer. But you can enhance your offer by adding any (or all) of the following:

1. Set a deadline

Rather than buying it 'someday' you want them to buy it 'right now'. So tell them why they should buy it now rather than later. Having a limited number of spots, closing registration after a certain number of days and offering a time-sensitive bonus or upgrade are all ways to set a deadline.

2. Emotional story

If you reach your customers on an emotional level, your message will be more powerful.

This point is also worth keeping in mind when following people up. Instead of asking what they *think* about your offer, ask them how they *feel* about it.

If you ask them what they think, they'll give you a logical answer. But if you ask them how they feel about it, you'll be able to tap into their emotions.

An existing customer talking about your product is far more powerful than you talking about it.

3. Logic

Occasionally you'll encounter 'spreadsheet buyers'—the accountant types who pull all the facts, figures and numbers together before they make a purchase.

Give them a logical reason to buy your offer, such as a guaranteed ROI (return on investment) figure.

4. Proof

You've said all this stuff about your offer. But can you prove it? This is where an existing customer talking about it (i.e. in a client testimonial) is far more powerful than you talking about it.

5. Trust

Can you include a certificate of authenticity or security seal? These kinds of trust elements will enhance any offer. Testimonials from previous customers will also help potential buyers trust you more.

6. Desire

Have you built desire?

If I'm looking at surfboard reviews, I want to see the board from all angles. I want to know what options I can get with it. I want to see it being ridden in the water. I want to know the dimensions. I want to know which superstar surfers use it. These can all help build desire.

Show me video of the product in use. Let me use it, or at least imagine myself using it.

In summary

Focus on creating an offer that converts, and you'll make your business transition faster and smoother than most other business owners.

Park your ideas to the side until you validate your market with an offer people will pay for. When you find an offer that converts, you'll have discovered the closest thing business has to a holy grail.

Think of Apple. After almost a decade and $100 million invested in the failed Newton, they eventually found an offer that converts. As I write this, Apple has sold 46.68 million iPhones. They changed the game for Apple, and continue to scale as fast as the market can consume them.

How to have a SPIN conversation

How do you know whether someone needs what you're selling them? Have a conversation with them, and employ the SPIN technique.

I learned this sales methodology (developed by Neil Rackham) at around the same time as my first sales role. SPIN stands for:

- Situation
- Problem
- Implications
- Needs (Solution)

A SPIN conversation involves asking questions and taking a genuine interest in the customer. Here's what you'll find out:

What's their SITUATION?

Why are they looking for a solution? Before finding the website-building software XsitePro, my situation was that I had a new business and no website.

What's their actual PROBLEM?

Sometimes the person thinks they have problem x when they actually have problem y. If you offer them something that solves problem x, you're doing them a disservice. (And

*It's your role to ask
questions that get to the
bottom of what their
real problem is.*

doing yourself a disservice, because you'll never see them again.)

It's your role to ask questions that get to the bottom of what their real problem (and thus pain) is.

When I had a new business and no website, my main pain was I didn't have any money to pay someone else to build one for me. So I tried doing it myself and found it very frustrating.

What are the IMPLICATIONS for the person if they don't solve this problem?

The implications of having no website for me was people wouldn't be able to find me online. Which is a problem when you're trying to start an online business.

What are the person's NEEDS?

What will actually solve their problem? The people selling XsitePro would have been rubbing their hands together with glee if they'd heard me say, 'If only there was software that people with no coding skills could use to build a website that looked good and worked well'.

That last bit of the SPIN conversation is the best bit. If your solution is right for the customer, they'll tell you how your product/service benefits them. They're basically writing and delivering your sales copy for you. And ordering from you without any pressure because they know they'll be better off.

SCAMPER Framework

The SCAMPER framework (named by Bob Eberle from some questions Alex Osborn developed) is a creativity tool that helps you come up with new ways to get results. You could use this tool to bring new life to a stale offer, or turn a flabby idea into a firm offer.

Ask yourself:

- Can you **Substitute** materials, resources or rules in your product?
- Can you **Combine** things differently? You know, like a waterproof camera and a mount. (GoPro.)
- Can you **Adapt** something, and use it in a different way to what it was designed for? Once they put cameras into phones no-one needed those tiny digital cameras anymore.
- Can you **Modify**, change the shape, or distort things slightly?
- Can you use something for another **Purpose**, or in a way you hadn't previously thought of? Coconut oil used to be a cooking ingredient. Now it's used in body scrubs and all kinds of crazy things.
- Can you **Eliminate** something to make it better?
- Can you **Re-arrange** or Reverse elements?

When you apply these ideas to what you currently offer, you'll be surprised at what you can achieve. I had a client whose offer was making him $30,000 a month. After doing an inventory of his assets (talents, skills and access to a particular market) he modified it and turned it into something new. Using a particular technique he was very good at, he helped his clients achieve real results.

Within a month he went from making $30,000 a month to making $300,000 a month. It was crazy.

Chapter 5 Action Items

- ❏ List potential markets you have access to.
- ❏ List products or services they are already buying.
- ❏ Shortlist one for research.
- ❏ Create your offer.
- ❏ Offer it to someone and collect payment.
- ❏ Create your low-resolution solution.
- ❏ Deliver it.
- ❏ Scale your offer.
- ❏ Refine your offer.

MORE READING/LISTENING

Visit JamesSchramko.com for a secret bonus chapter plus a list of recommended resources and additional notes that expand on this topic.

CHAPTER 6
Cash Flow and the Profit Formula

I couldn't believe it.

Five months after quitting my dealership job, I'd run out of money.

Christmas was imminent, and I had nothing to buy my kids presents with.

Given I'd only quit because my online income was matching my dealership income, I couldn't quite figure out how it had happened. After all, my advertising was strong and converting.

But, after a bit of digging, it all became clear.

At the time, I was making most of my money through affiliate sales. I'd spend my money upfront to generate leads for the sales, and then a month or two later the person I was an affiliate for would pay my commission.

The first problem was the significant lag between making a sale and getting paid for it.

The second problem, unique to this particular situation, was far worse. I'd managed to sell so much of one person's physical product, they couldn't actually deliver on it. (Unlike digital products that have no capacity constraints, physical products have many risks, including manufacturing and logistics.) A lot of people asked for refunds and the supplier went out of business.

The person I was an affiliate for owed me $16,000, but I never got paid.

It was a hard lesson to learn: making a lot of sales doesn't necessarily equate to good cash flow. Getting paid quickly is very important.

What is cash flow?

Cash flow is the money moving into and out of your business. It comes in from customers paying your invoices, and goes out as you pay your rent, staff costs and other expenses.

If there's more money coming in than going out then your business has a positive cash flow. And that's good. It means you have surplus funds, which can be saved for slow times (to protect your business), or invested to improve the business.

But if there's more money going out than coming in then you have a negative cash flow. And that's bad.

Very bad.

Negative cash flow is generally caused by two things:

1. **Slow paying customers:** If you pay your suppliers/expenses on time, but your customers don't pay you on time (or don't pay you at all), this causes cash flow pressure.

2. **Not enough profit in the business:** If you're just breaking even or worse, spending more than you're making and creating a loss in your business, again you'll be under cash flow pressure.

Why does negative cash flow impede your ability to work less and make more? It makes you overly reactive to what is (or isn't) showing up in your bank balance.

- When there's plenty of money in the bank, you may cruise a little in your business because there's no sense of urgency or financial pressure. You may even be tempted to spend it. Bad habits breed in good times.

- When there's no money in the bank, there's a good chance you'll panic. You'll start working all hours, and doing anything and everything to make a dollar. Things get desperate. And desperate times make for poor decision making.

How can you smooth things out? By understanding these **five eternal truths about cash flow.**

What's the best way to ensure you have money now and not later? By getting paid upfront for everything.

1. Money now is better than money later

The experience I had that first Christmas became the catalyst for me to change my entire business model. Since then I've consistently averaged more than $100,000 per month in income.

I'll be talking more about that in the following chapters. But in the meantime, what's the best way to ensure you have money *now* and not later?

By getting paid upfront for *everything*.

- When I provided SEO services, people paid in advance.
- When people join my online mastermind community, they usually pay for a year upfront.
- My high-performance coaching is six months upfront.
- When I run a live event, I get paid first and then I run the event.

You may not think your industry will allow for upfront payments. (I hear it from my coaching clients all the time.) *Test the assumption.* You'll be surprised by what people will do if you're firm and confident in your approach. You can set your own rules and choose what game to play.

Think about what you pay for in advance. For example, many cafes take your money and give you a number before they'll prepare and serve your meal. They don't want to risk you doing a runner.

Retraining your customers to understand they need to pay for your services before you perform them may take some effort. But the long-term gain will be worth it.

2. Money in your wallet is better than money a customer owes you

I understand that sometimes it simply isn't possible to get paid upfront (e.g. if you're working on government contracts). If that's the case, I strongly suggest you reconsider your business model so you don't have to service those kinds of clients because *you can't count on money that's owed to you.*

You can run cash flow projections based on when you *expect* to be paid. But you need to be incredibly conservative with your estimates. If you accept credit (i.e. perform services before they're paid for), you should allow for bad debts. Debt collection is big business because so many people default on their payments.

If you *still* accept payment terms, add an extra margin to cover collections and bad debts.

3. Having money in the bank doesn't mean you can spend it

A common cash flow killer is when people spend money simply because it's sitting in their account. Then a big bill arrives, and they have nothing to pay it with.

This cycle of spending money 'because it's there' and then having nothing in the bank to pay tax, wages and bills can be incredibly stressful.

How do you extract yourself from this cycle? By running regular profit and loss reports. (I have my team send me one every ten days.) Those will show you how your income and costs are tracking, and the profit that's available. They'll also tell you how much money you need to set aside for tax, wages and other upcoming expenses.

4. Hourly pricing means you probably have a job, not a business

I always feel for contract drivers when they're taking me somewhere because they're only getting paid while they're driving. When they stop driving, they stop getting paid.

Contrast this with the car owner who's leasing it to the driver. They're still getting paid even if they sit at home and play on their PlayStation.

Which is why you should sell your services, results or products *on a basis other than time.*

If you *do* sell time, make sure it's someone else's. It's okay to sell by the hour as long as you're not the one doing the fulfilling or delivering.

What's the alternative to hourly pricing? Value pricing. It's a way to provide leverage and build your profit. Think about what something is worth to the customer and then charge less than the end result.

When you introduce
value-based pricing
to your business
operations, it stops
being a job and
becomes a business.

Here's an example.

I paid a property buyer's agent $10,000 to make some phone calls and research a property I wanted to buy. His team performed the research, and then he met with the selling agent for an hour.

I ended up saving $105,000 on the purchase.

The agent spent about three hours on the job all up. His EHR was probably $2500 after paying costs and his team's wages. He got paid well for his knowledge, and the price seemed low to me given how much money I saved.

Here's another example.

Let's say an accountant wants a new website. If the designer quotes by the hour, they might charge for 40 hours at $100/hour, which is $4,000 all up.

But what if the designer knew each client brings in $15,000 worth of business to the accountant? They could set that as the price instead, and say, 'This website only needs to bring in one new client to pay for itself'.

When you introduce value-based pricing to your business operations, it stops being a job and becomes a business. One you'll enjoy more, and can potentially sell in the future.

5. Recurring income can be wonderful

Imagine selling something once, and then getting paid over and over again. That's the beauty of the recurring income model.

It's also an extremely stable way to build a business. Large companies such as Google, Apple and Amazon all have recurring income programs, and that cash flow stability lets them reinvest and grow bigger.

Recurring income supports fast growth. Knowing what your income will be in the coming months and years means you can confidently invest in teams and technology to take your business to the next stage. You can invest more to gain a customer than your competition, which will give you an increasing advantage.

The Profit Formula

There's one more eternal truth about cash flow I want to share.

If your business is incredibly profitable, you'll never have to worry about cash flow ever again.

How do you make your business more profitable? By focusing on improving the right numbers in the profit formula, which looks like this:

Prospects x Conversions = Customers

Customers x Price x Frequency x Margin = Profit

To get **customers,** you need **prospects** (also called 'leads').

Conversions turn prospects into customers.

When you take those customers and multiply by the product **price,** the **frequency** of transaction and the percentage **margin,** you end up with **profit.**

To increase profit we can:

- Get more prospects
- Convert more prospects into customers
- Increase our prices
- Sell more often (with up-sells, down-sells, cross-sells or recurring sells)
- Reduce costs.

A big mistake most business owners make is focusing too heavily on *reducing costs.* While it seems obvious, and is relatively easy to do, you can only reduce your costs by 100%. After that, there's nothing more to gain.

The next thing most people focus on is *increasing prices.* This usually produces a quick and easy win and, given most business owners aren't charging enough, is entirely warranted.

But there's a limit on how much you can increase your prices. And so once you've adjusted your price, you need to focus on the profit formula's more powerful metrics.

The second sale
is always easier
than the first.

1. Improving conversions

A typical online conversion rate is measured as a single digit. But there are a lot of things you can do to take a 1-2% conversion rate up to 5-15%.

1. Answer your phone faster.
2. Conduct sales training with every staff member.
3. Make your sales offer more compelling and relevant.
4. Offer a guarantee.
5. Use testimonials, case studies and demonstrations.
6. Talk about the benefits a prospect can expect rather than just features.
7. Include 'other customers bought' recommendations.
8. Use video and images to engage visual buyers.
9. Speed up your website, and make it easier to use.
10. Improve your follow-up after first contact.
11. Continually benchmark your best sales results.
12. Test multiple versions of the sales offer.

2. Increasing sales frequency

The second sale is always easier than the first. Most businesses focus on finding new customers, despite it being easier selling to a person who's already bought something from them. This is an easy win for existing business.

So, how do we increase frequency?

I used to sell a standalone product for $79. I decided to merge that product into an online forum community, and price that community at $79/month. It was a better solution for the customer because they could get support and further education from me and other customers. On average, people stayed in that community for 26 months.

$$26 \times \$79 = \$2,054$$

Receiving $2,054 instead of $79 was a profit increase of $1,975 (2,600%).

Another way to increase frequency is to add another offer to any purchase (known as an upsell).

- Someone buying face cream might also want a face massager.
- Someone buying a will might also want life insurance.
- Someone buying the first book in a series might want all three.

The opportunities for making additional offers to customers you already have are endless. My favourite way of doing this is the recurring subscription revenue model, which I'll talk about more in Chapter 8.

How to apply the Profit Formula to EHR

Remember, there are three ways to increase your EHR:

- Work fewer hours
- Make more money
- Both of the above

Leveraging the Profit Formula takes care of the second item in that list. Let's see it in action.

Take this scenario:

100 leads per day x 2% conversion = 2 customers
2 customers x $100 product x 1 time x 50% margin = $100 profit

Now, let's increase our smallest number (frequency) first.

100 leads per day x 2% conversion = 2 customers
2 customers x $100 product x 2 times x 50% margin = $200 profit

As you can see, doubling this number immediately doubles our profit.

Now, let's increase our conversions (the next smallest number) to 5%.

100 leads per day x 5% conversion = 5 customers
5 customers x $100 product x 2 times x 50% margin = $500 profit

Those two small changes have increased our profit by $400 (or 500%). And we haven't even touched our leads, price or margin yet.

*Imagine the impact
if you increased your
profits by 500% or
even 1,000%
this year?*

Improving these numbers is easy and fun.

In Chapter 3 I mentioned the power of focus, and how 4% of your actions deliver 64% of your results. Improving the small numbers in the Profit Formula is a definite 4% task, and one that can lead to significant gains in your business.

Imagine the impact if you increased your profits by 500% or even 1,000% this year?

What would that mean for your business, your family and your life?

A fun exercise

When I'm driving with my son Jami, we often play the Profit Formula game. We'll see a business vehicle in front of us—decked out with all its details—and brainstorm what the business could do to increase their profit.

For example, if it was a plumbing van they could:

- get **more leads** by running advertising or increasing the signage on the vehicle.
- convert **more sales** by training their telephone operator with sales scripts.
- **sell higher ticket items** by using high quality products and educating the customer about longer lasting, superior quality suppliers.
- **make more sales to existing customers** by leaving refrigerator magnets and sending a

follow-up letter after the job asking for referrals, or offering a 10% off coupon for the next job within a specific deadline.

- **increase their margins** by reviewing their bill payments for the previous year and asking for a better deal. They might be able to buy in bulk or negotiate a better hardware supply contract with a buying group.

Sound like a fun game to you?

Try it yourself next time you're out in public. Here's a Profit Formula template to get you started:

LEADS

- Add more sources where you collect prospects from (traffic channels)
- Increase each traffic channel effort
- Change the mix within channels
- Start a referral program
- Have promotion partners who will send you prospects for a commission (affiliates)

PRICES

- Add more value
- Target better customers
- Research your competition and look for gaps to fill
- Bundle multiple products
- Segment by specialty
- Add guarantee and risk reversal
- Offer a comparison chart
- Place in better environment (positioning)

MARGIN

- Ask your current supplier for a better deal
- Change supplier
- Reduce affiliate payouts
- Switch traffic sources
- Have stock on consignment if possible (versus buying it upfront)
- Joint venture with people who have what you need
- Piggyback items together (such as sending a promotion inside an invoice)
- Scale to reduce fixed costs per unit

CONVERSIONS

- Improve your sales offer wording (copywriting)
- See which of your traffic sources converts sales the most
- Test multiple versions of your sales offer (split test)
- Show different offers
- Segment prospects into smaller categories for relevance
- Conduct sales training
- Have professional design

FREQUENCY

- Add a recurring option
- Have a retention program including excellent first impressions
- Create a follow up sequence for people who visit your marketing but do not buy yet (abandonment sequence)
- Encourage consumption of the thing you sell
- Get results for people
- Schedule follow-ups more often

The fastest way to eliminate cash flow stress and boost your EHR is to increase your profit.

Summary

A business constantly experiencing cash flow stress will never be one where you can work less and make more. The fastest way to eliminate cash flow stress and boost your EHR is to increase your profit. And the fastest way to increase your profit is to make sure you have an offer that converts, and then increase the small numbers in the Profit Formula first.

Chapter 6 Action Items

- ❑ Get a profit and loss report sent to you every ten days.

- ❑ Run your best-selling product through the Profit Formula. Which number would be easiest to increase? Identify what you can do to increase it and then execute.

MORE READING/LISTENING

Visit JamesSchramko.com for a secret bonus chapter plus a list of recommended resources and additional notes that expand on this topic.

CHAPTER 7
Customer Lifetime Value

Gerry unfolded his copy of the stock sheet, which showed the price and margin of each car in our showroom.

He then pointed out the cars with the biggest margins—the oldest cars in stock that would make the most commission.

From that point on, whenever a customer entered the showroom Gerry directed them towards the cars with the biggest bonus. He didn't care whether or not they suited the customer's needs. He just wanted to make the most lucrative sale possible.

This is one reason the car industry has such a bad name.

It's also short-sighted. Why would you want to make only one sale to any given person? It's much easier to make repeat sales to people who have bought something from you before. You just need to deliver enough value on the first sale that they'd like to do business with you again.

Gerry didn't make many repeat sales.

I decided early in my car sales career that I wanted customers for life, not just for one sale. So when someone walked into the showroom, I'd talk to them, and find out what their car needs were. Then I'd show them the car that would best meet those needs. I didn't care about the commission. I only cared about finding the right vehicle for them.

And the funniest thing happened.

Those people would be so happy with their car that they'd come back and buy another, sometimes much sooner than the typical 28-month car purchasing life. Some even came back the following week.

They'd buy a car for their partner. They'd tell their friends in the office, and send their family members to me. Some ordered several cars for their first purchase.

I became 'their car guy'.

Within two years, half of my sales came from either existing customers or referrals.

This was rare in the car industry, and explains how, in one month, I managed to outsell all the other salespeople from my dealership *combined*.

When you look after someone and consistently provide value to them, it takes much less effort and investment to maintain that relationship than it does to find a new customer. Creating products for people who already know, like and trust you is very profitable.

In effect, you spend the most energy making the first sale. After that, you're simply maintaining the relationship and providing more and more value. And when you're selling to the same person again and again, the value of sales per customer increases dramatically.

The flawed 'ascension' model

There's a big problem in the marketing space. It's called the 'ascension' model, and leads to businesses losing high-value customers up front.

Many marketing sequences (often called funnels) don't take the time to understand the needs of each person coming to you. It lumps them all together, and forces them to run through the same steps in order:

1. Give someone a free report.

2. Offer them a low-cost product.

3. Offer a product that costs slightly more.

4. Offer an expensive product, perhaps with a recurring element to it.

5. Offer your most exclusive and expensive product.

In theory, this model will create lifetime customers for you. They start with something small, and then as they grow they can afford your next offer.

Fewer products and services can often be far more profitable.

But there are two problems with this approach:

1. It assumes every prospective customer has exactly the same (low-level) needs when they first come to you. (They don't.)

2. You always need to offer a range of products at a range of price points.

Pure madness.

If someone comes to me and sees immediate value in my highest priced product, I won't force them to download my free podcast and then work their way through the 'ascension' model. I'll let them access my most valuable offering straight away.

And who wants to be locked into providing a range of products and price points forever? Fewer products and services can often be far more profitable. If you want to be Rolex, you don't need to offer $10 watches. $10,000+ is more your market.

Is there a better model for creating lifetime customers? Yes.

The Chocolate Wheel approach

One of the smartest businesses I ever worked in combined a car dealership and a repair shop. This meant we could:

- Sell vehicles
- Finance vehicles
- Service vehicles
- Provide parts for vehicles
- Repair vehicles
- Insure vehicles

It was basically a license to print money because the opportunities for cross-promotion were insane.

This environment for cross-selling opportunity led me to create a model I call the Chocolate Wheel.

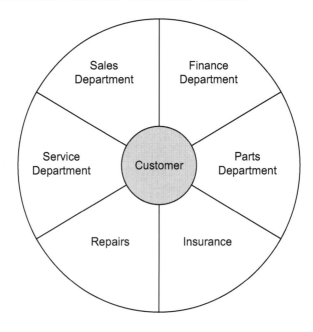

Instead of forcing customers to work their way through each step in a marketing funnel, I saw value in placing customers at the centre and making *every* product available to them.

Once all the managers in the business were on board with this approach, we created ways to move people between the departments seamlessly. We put point of sale material in the service department recommending new vehicles. When we sold a car, we'd go through a checklist from the parts department.

- Would you like carpet mats with your vehicle?
- Would you like a tow bar?
- Would you like tinted windows?

This approach greatly increased the lifetime value of our customers. We were solving all of their problems (not just the ones they came to see us about), and we weren't locking them into the linear funnel everyone loves so much.

When someone brought their vehicle in to have it serviced, someone from sales would value their car. Then someone in finance would work out if they could buy a new car for less than the monthly payments they were making on the current car.

The customer was always delighted with that.

The customer came in for a $50 petrol cap, he drove out with an order for a $330,000 SL500.

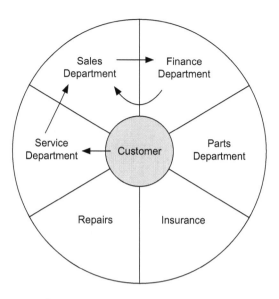

A mature gentleman once came to the parts area looking for a new petrol cap to replace his old one. While there, we recommended he have a look in the new car showroom. Despite coming in for a $50 petrol cap, he drove out with an order for a $330,000 SL500. (Yes, cars are really expensive in Australia.)

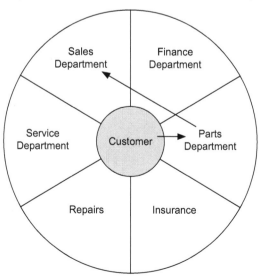

But what if you deal in services rather than products?

Instead of inviting people to join your email list (the first step in most ascension-type funnels), you can offer a chooser.

I did this on one of my first websites, and still do it on my coaching website.

When a visitor first comes to my site, I invite them to answer a couple of short questions about their current situation:

Question one is, 'How can I help you?'

They can choose from:

- I'm not sure how much to charge, or which business model is best for me.
- I'd like to improve my sales and conversion skills.
- I'm getting overloaded, and lack routine.
- My business is growing, and I need to hire and train a team.

Question two is, 'Which profit zone are you in right now?'

They choose from:

- Not quite $10K/year
- Somewhere between $10-200k/year
- More than $200K/year

How they answer those questions determines which product I present them with:

- Something free (such as podcasts, blog posts or online training)
- Something affordable (like my SuperFastBusiness coaching community)
- Something at a higher level (my SilverCircle coaching community)

Can you see how crazy it would be for me to tell someone who's ready to engage with me at SilverCircle level, 'Hey, why not subscribe to my free podcasts?'

Here's what a coaching business Chocolate Wheel might look like:

Cultivating customers who'll keep buying from you is a worthwhile pursuit.

While a typical path for a customer would be to attend my live event, then access my coaching services, then move to high-performance coaching, they can enter my coaching 'ecosystem' at whatever spot best suits their needs at the time.

When I look after them with integrity, they'll keep moving around the products in my business ecosystem depending on what they need.

The power of understanding Customer Lifetime Value

Cultivating customers who'll keep buying from you is a worthwhile pursuit.

It's time to calculate your average customer's lifetime value. Knowing that figure allows you to make good decisions about how you spend your time.

Customer Lifetime Value is what a customer is worth over the entire time they deal with you. It takes into account things such as the average purchase amount and how many times they purchase.

As an example, if a typical customer spends $1,000 with you three times, they're a $3,000 customer. If it costs you $1,500 to service that customer or provide them with a product, the customer profit is $1,500.

This means you can safely invest $500 to bring this customer into your business, knowing it will net you $1,000.

This is powerful when it comes to increasing your EHR.

Let's take the example of a bookkeeper. Their typical customer will:

- Pay: $250 per month
- Stay for: 36 months
- Cost: $100 per month (to service)

The bookkeeper knows each new client she brings into her business is worth (on average):

$$(\$250 \times 36) - (\$100 \times 36) = \mathbf{\$5400}$$

Imagine if that bookkeeper stopped spending ten hours a week messing around in Facebook and LinkedIn groups, and instead spent an hour a week reaching out to her own clients or complementary business owners.

What if she offered a $500 finder's fee to anyone who sent new clients her way?

What if that same bookkeeper spent five of the nine hours she saved each week creating a higher-priced offering for clients with higher-level needs? What if she converted 25% of her clients to that higher-level offering within a year and increased their customer profit from $5,400 to $10,000?

Imagine the impact these simple improvements would have on her EHR!

Remember: It's usually more effective to retain existing customers and help them buy more (particularly higher-cost offerings from you) than it is to find new customers.

One more thing. When you provide excellent value to your existing customers and they get results, they generally do the selling for you. This lets you work on ways to increase how often they purchase from you, and what they're willing to pay.

Chapter 7 Action Items

- ❑ Think of the different things your customer could experience in your business and present it on a simple products page.

- ❑ If you have a lot of offers, have a chooser that helps people find the right product.

- ❑ Take it the next step by figuring out the marketing channels you can use to direct people straight to the product they need today.

- ❑ Set up a cross-referral program to make sure your customers know how else you can help them.

MORE READING/LISTENING

Visit JamesSchramko.com for a secret bonus chapter plus a list of recommended resources and additional notes that expand on this topic.

CHAPTER 8
Choosing the Right Business Model

Not all business models are created equal. And most people I deal with are using the wrong one (with regard to being able to work less and make more).

What's the fastest way to determine whether yours is bad?

Ask yourself, 'Does it limit what I can earn?'

Here are two quick examples of models that limit your earnings:

1. Selling your time for money

A traditional job is a common example of selling your time for money. You sell 40-50 hours a week to your employer for $1,000-$2,000.

Having your own business gives you one advantage— you're building yourself an asset. But if you charge by the hour you have a problem: you only get 24 of those hours each day. And there's a limit on how many of those hours you can work without destroying every relationship you have and annihilating your health.

There's also a limit on how much you can charge for those hours (your hourly rate) before the market thins out significantly.

2. Selling lifetime access to a product

This is a surprisingly common but dangerous business model.

What does 'lifetime' mean? Your lifetime? The customer's lifetime? The lifetime of the product?

Imagine you paid $1,000 for 'lifetime access' to something and three years later it's discontinued? The seller no longer supports it and shuts it down. You'd be pretty unhappy, right?

Lifetime products create an ambiguous service debt and severely limit your income potential. While it might be nice to get all that money up front, you now have to deliver indefinitely. And the potential for creating unhappy customers is huge.

Another issue is that once you've sold lifetime access, there's rarely anything else you can sell to your customer.

So, what's a better business model?

Remember this from my introduction?

> *I work just a few hours a day.*
> *No #hustle.*
> *No weekly selling webinars or online summits.*
> *No stress-inducing, sleep-depriving, relationship-*
> *threatening once-a-quarter launches.*
> *Just a business model with smooth cash flow,*
> *predictable income, and the ability to do work that is*
> *meaningful to me.*

This chapter is all about that business model: **the recurring subscription model.**

Like many business owners, you probably think the key to financial success is having lots of customers. Yes, having many paying customers is good. But if each customer buys only one of your products or services, you need to spend a lot of resources finding new ones.

Happily, I have a solution to this.

Let's revisit the Profit Formula from Chapter 6.

Profit = Customers x Transaction Value x Frequency x Margin.

If your current frequency is one, and you double it to two, you've just doubled your profit. Now imagine if each customer buys from you not just once or twice, but six times, ten times, or a dozen?

When your existing
customers are paying a
set amount each month,
you're highly motivated
to ensure they never
have a reason to leave.

This is what the recurring subscription model does.

Here's an example.

A famous marketer I know was selling lifetime subscriptions to a $2,000 product. I suggested he switch from that lifetime model to a recurring annual subscription. That one change added $30,000 a month to his income. Instead of customers paying him once and him never making any further income from them, he now offers a solution that benefits both him and his customers. The following explains how.

Benefits of the recurring subscription model

1. It's a high value model

When your existing customers are paying a set amount each month, you're highly motivated to ensure they never have a reason to leave. So you work hard to provide ongoing value and nurture the relationship you have with them.

Because this model gives you more time and cash flow to refine your existing products, the customer also gets more value for the price they paid.

The more value the customer gets, the more likely they'll stick around and keep renewing their subscription. The longer they stick around, the more value they get. (And the less time you need to spend on finding new customers.)

2. Your customers have to actively stop you billing them

If a customer needs to contact you to discontinue the service you are providing, they can't do so mindlessly. They have to put some thought into explaining why they don't want or need your service any more.

If you provide a great service that solves a genuine problem, they'll usually realise, upon reflection, that staying with you offers access, certainty and stability. So they stay.

3. It builds on itself

The recurring subscription model is like an orchard or vineyard. You can keep refining and improving the process while it continually bears fruit.

4. It reduces stress

The consistent, reliable income that comes from a recurring subscription customer base lets you sleep well at night. You don't need to worry about what the coming months will bring, or how you'll survive the next round of expenses. You'll be able to accurately predict your profits for months ahead.

5. You can manage growth better

Stable, recurring subscriptions make it easy to compare how many customers leave with how many arrive and stay (your churn rate). If your business is expanding, you can get the right staff and systems in place to deal with it comfortably.

So long as you manage your available resources, and grow them as your subscriptions grow, there's no limit on how much you can earn.

6. It gives you leverage

Having a steady and reliable customer base means you can get better deals and set higher profit margins on supplies for your business.

When I supplied SEO services on a recurring subscription I could confidently hire a labour force without having to worry about letting people go the following month.

7. It's applicable to most industries

Subscription models can be adapted to work in almost every industry—from surfboard shops through to florist services.

8. It increases the lifetime value of your customers

Since you've read Chapter 7 you already know the power of this.

A recurring income business is simply one that provides a solution over and over again.

So, what exactly is a recurring income business?

A recurring income business is simply one that provides a solution over and over again.

Here are some examples:

A done-for-you service

For almost a decade I provided Search Engine Optimisation (SEO) services to business owners who weren't skilled in SEO and/or weren't interested in doing it themselves.

But they knew how important Google rankings were to the success of their business. They had a problem, and I had a monthly recurring service that provided a solution and added value to their business.

Before I sold it, this business was generating more than a million dollars a year. Businesses like this can be sold with higher multiples of profit because the income is predictable.

Win-win.

Other examples include the person who mows your lawn every two weeks, the bookkeeping service you have on a long-term monthly billing arrangement, and the internet service provider (ISP) that lets you access the web for a monthly recurring fee.

Software as a Service

Xero, Slack, Dropbox, Basecamp, Amazon Web Services and G Suite are all cloud-based services that charge their customers a continuing access fee. And people are willing to pay that fee because it adds value to their business by saving time and increasing productivity.

Is creating a Software as a Service (SaaS) product something only cashed-up startups can do? No. James Rose, a member of the SuperFastBusiness membership community, had a product called Silver Siphon that did one simple thing: it integrated Stripe billing with the Xero accounting system. Customers paid James anywhere from $9-$29 a month for the service because it saved them hours every month.

A paid community

A popular model for recurring subscriptions is a paid community (where people pay a monthly fee to access resources, coaching, like-minded people ... or all three). My SuperFastBusiness and SilverCircle communities are examples of these.

The scope for paid communities is wide. You just need to find yourself a starving crowd.

- Kevin Rogers of Copy Chief has built a paid community that connects business owners with copywriters.

- Carly Jacobs has a community called Crochet Coach where people can learn how to crochet and access patterns and tutorials.

- Shane and Jocelyn Sams have memberships where teachers can access both each other and countless resources, including lesson plans.

- Jarrod Robinson's PE Geek community helps PE teachers use technology in the classroom more effectively.

- Brenton Ford's Effortless Swimming membership provides access to swimming training and personalised technique analysis.

How to create a subscription business

Over the years I've helped countless people create profitable recurring subscription businesses. Here are six steps to creating your own:

Step One: Research what your target audience is already consuming

Chances are your customers already buy memberships, services, utilities and software on a recurring basis. Observe them. Survey them. And then use that information to identify what you can either create for them or provide them with as an affiliate (i.e. you don't *have* to create your own product, you can sell someone else's recurring subscription for an ongoing commission).

*Think about the results
the customer wants,
and then identify the
easiest way to help them
achieve those results.*

Step Two: Identify the results your target audience want to experience

You might think that to provide results on a recurring basis you need to provide a lot of things. But this simply isn't true. The customer is only interested in *results*. Think about the results the customer wants, and then identify the easiest way to help them achieve those results.

Step Three: Create your offer

How will you solve your target audience's problem and help them get results?

That's your offer.

If you're able to provide a solution that will give your target audience the results they want *and* it's something they're already paying for in some way, you have a *compelling offer*.

Step Four: Validate it

Always make sure people are willing to pay for your subscription before building the delivery mechanism. This step allows you to avoid wasting effort and expense.

How did I know there was a market for my coaching services? Early in my online career I offered 60 days of bonus coaching to people who purchased someone else's high-cost product from me.

All up, 78 people purchased that high-cost product specifically to get access to my coaching. And I got paid an affiliate commission.

It validated the marketing for my coaching offering, which is still going strong.

Step Five: Build it

Get professional help to assemble the technology and infrastructure you need to deliver your customers' results. Typically, you'll need a database (or at least an email list) to track buyers, and a shopping cart or payment facility to collect money.

You'll also need a platform where you can deliver your results. It might be a private forum, a service scheduler, or a supply arrangement with a wholesale provider.

Step Six: Drive traffic

In the beginning, you'll probably need to drive traffic to your site. Here are some ways to do it:

1. PROVIDE TRAINING

You can deliver training live and online via paid workshops or seminars. At the end, offer the attendees a redeemable sample/trial or introduction to your subscription. This ensures you're only making your offer to qualified prospects who'll stay on if they like what they see.

2. PROVIDE A DIAGNOSTIC SERVICE

I did this for my SEO business, and you can easily adapt it to drive people to your offering. We charged people $20 to look at their website and provide a report on what state it was in, how well it was optimised, and what they should change.

We then said we'd credit the $20 towards any of our recurring SEO services. The diagnostic service was really effective for us, converting more than half the people who bought a report into an ongoing recurring program.

3. BE THE AUTHORITY

An effective way to do this is to set up an authority content website on your own domain (something I talk about in the bonus chapter available from my website).

You could also start a podcast. iTunes is a fabulous platform that gives people direct access to you, (and you to them) via their smart device. I've generated tens of thousands of downloads each month with my podcasts. They are a prime traffic source for my website.

4. PAID TRAFFIC

Facebook ads are getting more powerful every day, and the level of targeting you can do with them is insane. You can also do remarketing with AdWords.

Both paid traffic sources offer excellent value. However, I suggest either taking a course on this topic or hiring a professional paid advertising agency.

Most people who make money from books do so because they have a high-value product or recurring membership to sell.

5. PRESENTING

Presenting, whether it's on a stage or a webinar, can create a strong platform for selling subscriptions. Being 'up there' gives you instant credibility, and a captive, engaged and high-converting audience.

6. BOOKS

If someone has already bought your book and taken your teachings on board, what more can you offer them?

Hopefully your answer isn't just 'more books'.

Most people who make money from books do so because they have a high-value product or recurring membership to sell.

Many of my customers are experts, coaches, authors and others who weren't authorities in their fields when they started working with me. Once they set up an authority platform and attached a membership to it, however, their businesses transformed.

The importance of retention

I've heard that the industry standard retention rate for online communities is three months. This is mind-boggling to me. My active members stay for at least 30 months, and many have been with me since 2009.

Why? Because I focus hard on nurturing the customers I already have. It's much easier than finding new customers.

And when you do look after your existing customers, they become your unofficial sales force. Both of my membership waiting lists are topped up regularly with people referred by existing customers.

Here's how I look after those customers:

Weekly news updates

Most people take this approach with recurring billing: 'If we bill monthly, hopefully the customer won't notice it on their credit card and they'll stick around until they remember'. Those people don't want to send out weekly news because it keeps reminding subscribers that they're paying for something on a monthly basis.

I see my weekly emails differently; as a kind of long-line fishing. When I share the ten most popular topics being discussed in my forum community, that's like having ten hooks on a line. If someone clicks through to view one of those topics, they're consuming my information and engaging with others in the community. The more involved they are, the more likely they are to stay a member.

Always have something coming

Dean Jackson shared this tip with me a long time ago. I hold live masterminds once a month, live events most years, and regular meetups in major regional areas. I add new courses and training to the membership all the time, and my members get it before the public do.

Bottom line: There's always something new going on in my community to keep everyone engaged, excited, and focused on getting results.

Encourage loyalty

When your first batch of customers join up, give them a low rate because they're taking a risk on you. At the 30-day mark, increase the public rate but lock your first members into the 'founder's rate' (the lower rate).

Your entire membership now has a discount to the market rate. Each month will be a reminder that it's worth staying because if they leave and come back it will cost more.

This has a huge psychological effect. As you increase your price two or three times, you'll have members who are paying rates of 20%, 30% or even 40% less than new members.

Those people will stick around forever.

Offer a free trial period

This is something you should only do for qualified customers (i.e people who've already paid you money for something else), and with what I call 'optional forced continuity'.

As part of their 60-day free trial registration, have them agree that you can start billing them on day 61.

Having only one payment option could be preventing some customers from doing business with you.

Why? If they've already given you their payment details, when day 61 rolls around they don't have to decide whether or not to stay on. They already made the hard decision, (when they first gave you their credit card details).

But you must warn them prior to the first billing. That way you'll avoid the frustration of bank chargebacks, or hostile customers claiming you've billed them without permission.

Be very clear about this when they first sign up. Then, before the first billing attempt, make it very clear that you'll be billing them in a few days, and that they should let you know if they'd like to leave.

Offer multiple payment and billing options

Having only one payment option could be preventing some customers from doing business with you. Make sure you offer multiple payment options.

You should also consider different billing periods.

I prefer annual billing to monthly billing. Most experts tell you to have monthly billing because it lowers the risk to the customer. But while monthly payments make it easy for people to buy, they also attract customers who don't have a long-term view of doing business with you.

Annual billing also means you can downsell to six-monthly billing if someone really can't afford the annual amount. This bridges the gap, and still lets them invest with you. I've increased my EHR by increasing my minimum subscription term and raising prices.

Remember, it's not about stuff, it's about results.

People often think, 'Oh, I can't start a community until I have 100 videos in there'. Which means they start a year later than they could have, or sometimes not at all.

The customer doesn't care how much content there is. Remember, most people have too much stuff in their lives already.

They're not looking for content. They're looking for results.

I have a lot of content in my communities (because I've been building that content for ten years). When I bring someone new into the community, however, I point them only to the content that's relevant to their situation right now. If I pointed them to everything, they'd be paralysed into inaction.

Do the minimum you can to get a result for your customer. You might not have a lot of content in the early days of your membership. But you probably have a lot of time because you don't have that many people subscribed yet. Use that time to give more personalised attention to the people who are onboard, and help them get results fast.

Final word

The recurring subscription model can be a lot of work in the beginning. But once it's in full swing, there's no greater return on investment. The number of customers you can service in a one-to-many situation is high, while the costs involved tend to be the same whether you have one person or a hundred using the service.

You can liken it to a freight train. You might need to shovel a lot of coal to get it moving, but once it has momentum you can ease off and it will keep going.

Chapter 8 Action Items

❑ Research your target market. What are they already spending money on? Can you package up and provide something better?

❑ If you're a service-based business, would it help your clients to have you on retainer? They'll know what their monthly spend will be, and you'll know what your income and cash flow will be.

❑ Look at what you currently purchase on a recurring basis. Can you reverse engineer any of those models and make it work for you?

MORE READING/LISTENING

Visit JamesSchramko.com for a secret bonus chapter plus a list of recommended resources and additional notes that expand on this topic.

CHAPTER 9
No Compromise

Four years ago, Wilco de Kreij discovered the 'launch model' for doing business. The model looks something like this:

1. Create a compelling product or offering

2. Generate huge buzz around the product (via website opt-ins, videos, email sequences, Facebook ads, etc.)

3. Recruit joint venture partners who will promote it to their customers by email when the product launches

4. Provide those joint venture partners with sales material, and give them an incentive to sell as much of your product as they can. (It's usually a 50% commission on each sale, plus a promise to email your customers when they do their big product launch.)

5. Set up sales offer pages, and ensure your online payment systems are robust enough to handle a high volume of transactions

6. Open up your product for sale for four to six days only. (You'll need to be available to both affiliates and purchasers to answer questions, and to ensure your online systems haven't crashed. So you won't be getting much sleep.)

7. Enjoy the rewards of making six or seven figures in four to six days.

Sounds good, right?

After doing his first big launch, Wilco was hooked. Being able to generate huge amounts of revenue in a few days was hugely seductive.

He started doing them every six months.

Then one day, he was on day two of a launch when he got a phone call no-one ever wants to get. His wife had been in a bike accident.

He dropped everything and rushed to the hospital.

And that's when he discovered a major flaw with the launch model.

The huge amounts of money that can be made in those few days belie the months of work setting up the launch. Not to mention the effort and pressure involved in creating something new from scratch every six months.

Even a small problem during the launch can see months of work go up in flames. Your wife being in a bike accident is not a small problem.

While caring for his wife during her recovery Wilco came to a realisation:

This isn't a business model. It's a trap.

Personally, I'd use another word to describe it: **compromise.**

- Every launch requires a huge investment of time, energy and cash for returns that are not guaranteed.

- Successful launches are equivalent to a sugar rush, there's a massive comedown when it's all over.

- You end up with a 'feast or famine' cash flow. You have all this money coming in and then ... nothing.

- They create a surge and strain on customer support, which can have huge implications for your reputation. (If you bring in all these customers and can't support them properly, it can do a lot of damage to your brand.)

- A large chunk of income from each launch goes to affiliates, refunds and the experts you use to manage and drive the campaign. (It's not uncommon to net a mere 20% of the sales revenue.)

*As a business model,
big launches are a
perfect example of a
situation where big
dollars are offset by huge
compromises.*

- They create a lot of pressure and coercion in the marketplace, which creates stress for buyers and gives the marketplace launch fatigue.
- You have to keep your promise, and promote whatever your joint venture partners want to launch to your customers—even if you don't think the product is very good, or your customers don't need it.

Now, I'm not against big launches. I feel they are a great promotional tool.

As a *perpetual business model*, however, they are a perfect example of a situation where big dollars (which everyone focuses on) are offset by huge compromises (which everyone ignores).

Here are three other highly dangerous forms of compromise I've seen.

Sylvia Van de Logt runs a fashion website that generates income through advertising and affiliate links. Those earnings are highly dependent on her current traffic (400-500K visitors a month).

But 75% of that traffic comes from Google organic search. And if Google ever decides to blackball Sylvia's site (as it has done to many sites without notice), most of it will evaporate.

> *The compromise? Single-source dependency (over-reliance on any ONE thing).*

Ryan Levesque had a mastermind community with 2,000 members, who all paid $100 a month. A major drawcard of membership was getting access to the mastermind's Facebook group.

At his community's peak (when it was a $2 million a year business), Facebook shut down a number of similar high-profile groups without warning or recourse. A shudder went through Ryan's organisation. If the same happened to them, it would instantly wipe out both their reputation and their business.

> *The compromise? Building your house on someone else's land. Land you don't control.*

Kevin Rogers is a comedian turned copywriter. He spent ten years building his reputation and freelance writing business, and was in high demand.

But it didn't stop him being at the mercy of his clients. All his work involved high stress and tight deadlines, and he was always one lost client away from losing a big chunk of income (and having to hustle to replace it).

> *The compromise? Sacrificing physical and mental health.*

Compromise is optional

It's easy to think that compromise is part of any entrepreneurial venture. But you do have control over how much compromise you're willing to accept.

Too many business owners ignorantly or willingly tolerate levels of compromise I consider unacceptable.

- Working long hours and making sleep, fun, health and relationships low priorities.
- Saying 'How high?' when customers ask them to jump.
- Paying an expensive ego-driven office lease when they could just as easily run their business from home.
- Building their website on a platform they don't own, and can be taken down at any time (such as Wix or Squarespace).
- Never going on holiday because if they're away from their business for 24 hours everything falls apart.

The list is long, and potentially depressing. But it doesn't need to be that way.

Here are three things you can do to drastically reduce compromise in your business.

When you're deep in the weeds of running a business it's always tempting to take the easier option.

1. Question everything

Remember the Jarrod Robinson case study from Chapter 3? Jarrod was making a lot of assumptions about his business, which led to huge compromises.

- He compromised a rich and full life by assuming he needed to keep working as a PE teacher while running his PE Geek business on the side.
- He compromised his income by assuming he could only deliver workshops to 20 people at a time.
- He compromised the growth of his business by assuming he personally needed to run all of his workshops.

When we put these assumptions to the test, Jarrod discovered they didn't stand up. And when he removed these compromises from his business and his life, things really took off.

2. Do the hard thing

When you're deep in the weeds of running a business, or building a side hustle alongside a full-time job, it's always tempting to take the easier option.

- It's easier to keep an underperforming staff member than to go through the process of moving them on.
- It's easier to accept traffic from one source than develop a second one.

- It's easier to stay on the couch and watch three hours of Netflix than go to bed at a decent time.

But whenever we take the easy option, we create a compromise. And every compromise we make stunts the growth of our business and increases the number of hours we need to work.

While doing the hard thing might seem painful now, the long-term benefits to your business will make it worthwhile.

As a side note, this is why getting people to 64:4 their business operations and delete low-impact tasks from their days is so exciting. Those tasks drain your energy, and make doing the hard things … well, hard.

3. Mitigate risk

Take backups of your important business documents. It's not if your computer fails, it's when. I've had one laptop stolen and another suddenly stop operating. Fortunately, I operate mostly from the cloud. A quick trip to the Apple store on both occasions, and I was back in business.

What about platforms such as Facebook, where you might have 100,000 followers on a page or 10,000 members in a group? Facebook doesn't let you back up those 'lists'.

In that kind of situation, get as many of them as possible on to your email list. That way, if Facebook does delete your page one day you'll still be able to reach them.

The 'no-compromise approach' in action

Let's revisit my earlier examples of compromise, and see how a no-compromise approach allowed them and their businesses to thrive.

Sylvia Van de Logt saw the dangers of having 75% of her website's traffic coming from Google's organic search. To *mitigate that risk*, she:

- Built her email list up to more than 30,000 subscribers.
- Built social media followings on multiple sites: 20,000+ on Pinterest, 16,000+ on Instagram, 15,000+ on Facebook.
- Built a very active closed group on Facebook with 6,200 people in it.
- Added a membership component to her site that contributes $3,000 a month to her income, and is growing every day.

If Google ever fails her, she still can reach a large audience.

Ryan Levesque shut down the $2 million a year business he'd built on Facebook's platform. How did he ensure he'd never be in such a position again? *He did the hard thing.*

His company teaches a marketing methodology called the ASK method. Ryan wrote a book that shared his method, and used it to drive people to his online training. Wary of using other people's software packages (and those packages'

Kevin now has a strong mid-six-figure a year business with predictable income that lets him anticipate costs and always leave enough profit.

limitations) to deliver that training, Ryan's company built its own.

Then they discovered a need for technology to implement the ASK methodology, but nothing was available. So Ryan made the biggest investment of his life and built software that could do it.

Ryan now certifies marketing professionals to use both the software and his methodology. When people tell him 'I'd like to hire someone to implement ASK in my business', he can deliver on that demand.

He now has powerful control of the space he operates in.

Kevin Rogers was looking down the barrel of adrenal fatigue and constant burnout. And the one-to-one model was compromising his health.

I asked him to *challenge the assumption* that a one-to-many model wouldn't work for him. It wasn't a quick or easy process, but removing that assumption from the equation led to him building copychief.com—an online community for copywriters.

The effect on Kevin's business has been life-changing. He now has a strong mid-six-figure a year business with predictable income that lets him anticipate costs and always leave enough profit.

He's gone from:

- An unscalable commodity to a specialised recurring revenue machine.

- Obscurity to an authority and celebrity in his space.
- Being fearful to knowing there is no limit for his business.
- Being unknown to having people who matter calling him.
- Having to constantly hustle to having people knocking down his door.

A compromise you can tackle right now

When I first start working with coaching clients, I send them a long questionnaire to get a feel for where they're at, both in work and in life. And nearly all of them are making one destructive but easy to fix compromise:

They have a cavalier approach to sleep.

The idea that 'sleep is for the weak' is endemic among entrepreneurial types. It's the first thing people sacrifice when they feel overwhelmed. Before long, pulling all-nighters or surviving on four hours sleep a night in the pursuit of business and life goals becomes a habit. (The talking heads espousing this hustle and grind also have big racoon-like black eyes indicating sleep deprivation. I expect they'll have serious health concerns at some point.)

When your sleep is regularly compromised:

- Simple decisions become difficult.

- You have trouble distinguishing between the important and the trivial, and you wind up feeling overwhelmed.
- You're less likely to exercise regularly.
- You're always hungry. (Chronic sleep loss can wreak havoc on your sugar levels and reduce the production of leptin—the hormone that signals when you're full. Tired people also tend to gravitate towards sugars and simple carbohydrates—not exactly healthy food choices.)
- You get more colds. (Inadequate sleep increases your vulnerability to infections.)
- You become less emotionally stable. (And physically for that matter. Research has shown that people who don't get enough sleep have slow reflexes and less precise motor functions.)
- You make bad choices in your business.

Compromising on sleep can create a 'domino effect' of compromises through all areas of your life.

Aim to get one more hour of sleep per night than you're getting right now.

Set an alert to remind yourself to switch off at night. Ten o'clock worked well for me until it became a habit. (I also removed the blinds from my windows so I could wake up with the sun.)

*The fewer compromises
you're making in life,
the happier you'll be.*

Manage this one compromise out of your life, and you'll be stunned at the energy boost you get. You can then put that energy towards:

- Doing high-impact tasks in your business.
- Moving your EHR in the right direction.
- Identifying and then removing or mitigating all the compromises you're making in business and life.

If there's one thing I've learned in my years on this earth, it's that the fewer compromises you're making in life, the happier you'll be.

Chapter 9 Action Items

It's time to audit:

- ❑ What compromises are you making in your business that could be limiting you?

- ❑ What can you do to test and challenge assumptions you're currently making?

- ❑ Where are you giving up control?

- ❑ How can you take back that control?

- ❑ How can you mitigate the risks inherent in those compromises?

- ❑ Are you getting enough sleep currently? If not, set yourself a 'go to sleep' alarm each night and aim to get one more hour than you're getting currently.

MORE READING/LISTENING

Visit JamesSchramko.com for a secret bonus chapter plus a list of recommended resources and additional notes that expand on this topic.

CONCLUSION
It's All About Leverage

Once again, I'm at a conference. It's a different group to the one I mentioned at the start of this book, but my presentation is along similar lines.

As I share where I've gotten to today, someone pipes up in the audience.

'But, you've built up to that, right?'

'To being able to work a few hours a day, surf every day and achieve financial independence? Yes, that's right.'

'But, ten years ago—'

'Ten years ago, I didn't have 'today' me telling 'younger' me this stuff.'

If only I did have 'today' me ten years ago. I wouldn't have had to cram 30 years of business into ten, trying everything and working countless hours to get where I am today.

Remember what I said I was guessing about you in the Introduction?

1. You're currently working too hard for your money.
2. You're way ahead of where I was when I first started seeking financial independence.
3. You're overwhelmed and not sure where to start.

I can now add a fourth item to the list.

4. You have me.

That guy in that audience? There's one in every crowd. The person who looks for a reason why something won't work before they even try it.

Don't be that person. Be open to the possibility that the ideas in this book will help you rise faster, and live a better life.

Yes, it took me ten years or so to get to where I am today.

But I started at zero. I knew nothing. And I couldn't find anyone who had already achieved what I was trying to do.

My challenges then aren't your challenges now.

Today, the people I work with achieve stunning results in just one or two years because they can use my knowledge to their benefit.

And really, that's all this book is about. Leverage.

What is leverage?

Leverage is simply using something to its maximum advantage. Here are the three things I hope this book has taught you how to leverage appropriately.

1. Yourself

Back in **Chapter 1** (the one about personal effectiveness), the first thing I asked you to do was look in the mirror and resolve to take control of what your future looks like.

Why? Because you can't use yourself to maximum advantage if you put your destiny in the hands of others.

I then asked you to track your time—how you were spending your days, how many hours you were working, and the effect it was having on your EHR.

Why? Because EHR is measurable.

When you're staring at an EHR of $20 or less like many people, it's painful. But it also lets you see where you want to be.

You get to increase your EHR to $50.

Then $100.

Then $200 and way beyond. With the right approach, an EHR of $1,000 is certainly possible.

Chapter 2 showed how important it is to know where you're going because you can then lay down the tracks to get you there.

Success isn't being at the beach with your laptop.

In **Chapter 3** I showed you how to zero in on the 4% tasks in your business, the ones that deliver 64% of your results.

The goal of those first three chapters was to show you where you weren't using yourself to maximum advantage and, most importantly, provide firm action items for making the necessary changes.

2. Your team

Whenever I talk to clients about building a team, the most common response I get is eyes glazing over.

Most entrepreneurial types don't like managing people.

Worse, they usually perform at such a high level that all they can think is, *I really need another me. Where am I going to find another me?*

If you focused in **Chapter 4**, you know you don't need another you. If you can write out the steps for a task, or record yourself doing something on your computer, that task can be handed off to someone else. Even better, you can hire someone who can write out the steps for themselves. Yes, it's possible.

If you're still resisting the idea of a team, ask yourself, 'Could I go on a holiday without taking my laptop?'

So many people pride themselves on having a business they can take anywhere. Have you seen pictures of people lying in hammocks with a laptop?

Success isn't being at the beach with your laptop.
Success is being at the beach with your surfboard.

Holidays are a time to recharge and spend quality time with the people you love. But how can you recharge if you're working while on holiday?

There's also the mental load to consider.

These days, when I am on, I am ON. I can do that because when I'm off, I totally disconnect my brain and my body from work.

Who lets me do this? My team.

3. Your business

I'm glad you have a business (or are considering creating one). You can change your life far more easily as a business owner than you can as an employee.

Case in point. The simple act of reading this book and actioning one or two points means you can immediately change your EHR. As in today.

A job won't let you do that. A job doesn't care how personally effective you are. You'll still be expected to work the same number of hours. You'll still be paid the same salary. And chances are you can't duck off for a surf at lunchtime or watch a movie during the day like I do every day.

Here's what this book's covered with regard to leveraging your business.

Chapter 5 showed the importance of having an offer that converts—a solution to a problem that people are willing to pay for. Without a strong offer, you don't actually have a business.

Chapter 6 introduced you to the Profit Formula and showed which elements of that formula are easiest to increase; increases which significantly impact your bottom line.

Chapter 7 presented the concept of Customer Lifetime Value, and how important it is for a profitable and sustainable business.

Chapter 8 shared the most powerful model for leveraging both the Profit Formula and Customer Lifetime Value— the recurring subscription model.

Finally, in **Chapter 9**, we talked about removing compromise from your life and business. You learned how to ensure your income and lifestyle can never be yanked from underneath you on the whim of someone else (especially faceless multi-nationals such as Facebook and Google).

And now we're here, at the end of the book.

In my introduction I nominated EHR as 'the metric that matters' because it's easy to measure and easy to change quite dramatically, both immediately and in the long-term.

It's a quantifiable way to measure the impact of this book on your life.

I dare you to set something you LOVE as the thing you do every day.

But life satisfaction goes beyond formulas and figures. Which is why I want to wrap things up with a question.

And a dare.

What would you rather be doing?

About 15 years ago I was on my way home and saw people driving along with surfboards on the roof. I remember thinking, *How can they do that? I'm making all this money, and I'm so 'successful', and yet they're outside every day while I'm working 70-hour weeks. All I can do when I get home is collapse.*

Then in 2012 I moved to Manly—a beachside suburb in Sydney, Australia.

I liked the surf culture there. I liked the food they ate, and what they wore. I especially liked how chilled and relaxed they were.

Eventually I decided it was weird to live in Manly and not know how to surf. While on a trip to Hawaii, my friend Ezra Firestone took me surfing. When I got home, I borrowed a friend's board and continued learning to surf.

Doing this completely changed my life. It became a new baseline. A new filter for the decisions I made about business, and life. If something would get in the way of me surfing every day, I wouldn't do it.

I dare you to set something you LOVE as the thing you do every day.

And then I dare you to build your business to cater for it.

Why? Because if you're not doing something you love, you're not actually living.

Let go of the idea that when you turn 65 you'll stop doing whatever you're doing now and start spending your savings/superannuation to live the life you want.

Perhaps you can travel around the world now.

Perhaps you can do the thing you want to do now.

It doesn't matter whether it's knitting, or playing bingo, tennis, golf or whatever. I encourage you to start doing it now.

What you'll find is this: *When you do it every day, it will give you the energy you need to get things right.*

It will drive you to put the ideas and concepts in this book into action—to fully leverage yourself, your team and your business.

Best of all, it will ensure the journey is as much of a reward as any destination can ever be.

ACKNOWLEDGEMENTS

Bringing a book to life is a huge undertaking, and I have many people to thank.

Firstly, this book wouldn't have happened without Kelly Exeter. Kelly saw me present, and suggested I write the book. She then did all the heavy lifting needed to take things from initial idea to final manuscript; all while providing a huge amount of encouragement and advice.

A mountain of transcripts and resources was refined to what you see in this book. Large chunks of the writing and finessing came from her fingertips; her contribution was enormous.

I'm grateful to the members of my SuperFastBusiness and SilverCircle communities. The work I've done with them provided great nuance to the thoughts I share in this book. I'd particularly like to thank Jarrod Robinson, Wilco de Kreij, Sylvia Van de Logt, Ryan Levesque and Kevin Rogers for letting me share their personal stories.

Everyone knows books are judged by their covers.

Malcolm Lyons from Lyons Imagery took the cover shot, while Greg Merrilees and his team at Studio1 Design produced a final cover that has both style and impact. Kelly Exeter directed the concept and style. (Her team at Swish Design also designed the book's interior.)

Bill Harper from Sharper Copy did the line edits (any unnecessary adverbs and qualifiers that remain are mine, not his), while Kym Campradt had the enviable job of proofreading.

Ian Freestone and Adrian Crawford read the draft version of this book while we were floating around the Maldives, and provided insights and comments that were hugely valuable.

Finally, a massive thank you to my kids Jack, Jordan, Jamieson and Jensen. You're the motivation behind everything I do.

STAY IN TOUCH

If you want to find out more about the things I've shared in this book, head to JamesSchramko.com. You'll find a special bonus chapter there for you to download—one that details the approach I took to generate a steady stream of leads for all my businesses and ensure I was building saleable assets.

If you have thoughts or comments you'd like to share with me about the book, please email me on james@ jamesschramko.com.

You can also connect with me on:

> **Facebook:** facebook.com/Jamesschramko

> **Twitter:** @JamesSchramko

> **Instagram:** @JamesSchramko

Feel free to tag any mentions of this book with **#worklessmakemore**. Instagram is a great place to share pictures of you being at the beach *without* your laptop. #justsaying.

Made in the USA
San Bernardino, CA
06 March 2020